THE CREDO SERIES

VOLUMES ALREADY PUBLISHED

THE CREDO SERIES

PLANNED AND EDITED BY
RUTH NANDA ANSHEN

DIALOGUES

Reflections on God and Man

BY

PAUL VI

Translated and Arranged
By John G. Clancy

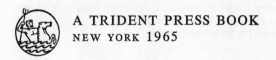 A TRIDENT PRESS BOOK
NEW YORK 1965

Prepared under the supervision of
POCKET BOOKS, INC.

LIBRARY OF CONGRESS CATALOG NUMBER: 65-13107
PUBLISHED SIMULTANEOUSLY IN THE UNITED STATES AND CANADA
BY TRIDENT PRESS
MANUFACTURED IN THE UNITED STATES OF AMERICA

To my friend, George Barry Ford, and with grateful appreciation to Sisters M. Stephanie, M. Mercedes, and M. Euphrasia of the Sisters of Mercy; and to several students of St. Joseph's College for Women, Standish, Maine for their invaluable assistance in the preparation of this manuscript.

—John G. Clancy

CONTENTS

CHRISTIANITY VIEWS THE WORLD:
MAN AND HIS SPIRITUAL DIMENSION
The Christian Predicament

THE CREDO SERIES

Its Meaning and Function

The Credo Series suggests that an epoch has come to an end, an epoch in which our best knowledge has been dimmed with boredom or darkened by destruction. We have felt for too long that this must be the very nature of life; this is the way life is, and to such a degree that life has consented to shrink from its own terrors, leading us to a deep apostasy of the heart and a crucifixion of our natural aspiration for experience and growth.

The absolute has surrendered to the relative. Our era of relativity, however, whether in science or in morals, does not allow us to assume that relativity implies an absence of ground to stand on, and therefore a relaxation of all effort toward foundations. "There is no firm ground," the dominant malaise of our time, this acceptance of non-finality, summons us to a heightened task. For the failure of formulated absolutes leaves the absolute requirement to evaluate again that uncaptured reality which contains and guides the total meaning of our existence.

The Credo Series hopes to unlock a consciousness that at first sight may seem to be remote but is proved on acquaintance to be surprisingly immediate since it shows the need to reconcile the life of action with the life of contemplation, practice with principle, thought with feeling, knowledge with being, and work, no longer a form of punishment as in the Judaeo-Christian tradition, but accepted as a way toward the growth and realization of the self in all its plenitude. For the whole meaning of self lies within the observer and its shadow is cast naturally on the object observed. The fragmentation of man from his work, the being of man into an eternal and temporal half, results in an estrangement of man from his creative source, from his fellows and from himself.

The symbol of *The Credo Series* is the Eye of Osiris. It is the inner Eye. Man sees in two ways: with his physical eyes, in an empirical sensing or *seeing* by direct observation, and also by an indirect envisaging. He possesses in addition to his two sensing eyes a single, image-making, spiritual and intellectual Eye. And it is the *in-sight* of this inner Eye that purifies and makes sacred our understanding of the nature of things; for that which was shut fast has been opened by the command of the inner Eye. And we become aware that to believe is to see.

Thus, it is suggested, there may be born a sharpened vision, which comes from seeing reality as the incarnation of associations and affinities with something beyond the visible self. For it is our hope to show the human relevance of ideas, the ways in which knowledge can help us to live in the immediate and real world by pointing to the confluence of man and his vocation, of subject and object, by reverencing the curious and mysterious metabolism between man and matter, the sacred nexus between the person and his work, and by asking whether the freedom now released through the creative energies of mankind will bring salvation or destruction, the answer to which will depend upon the aims we cherish.

The Credo Series submits that the universe itself is a vast entity where man will be lost if it does not converge in the person; for material forces or energies, or impersonal ideals, or scientifically objectified learning are meaningless without their relevance for human life and their power to disclose, even in the dark tendencies of man's nature, a law transcending man's arbitrariness.

For the personal is a far higher category than the abstract universal. Personality itself is an emotional, not an intellectual, experience, and the greatest achievement of knowledge is to combine the personal within a larger unity, just as in the higher stages of development the parts that make up the whole acquire greater and greater independence and individuality within the context of the whole. Reality itself is the harmony which gives to the component particulars of a thing the equilibrium of the whole. And while physical observations are ordered with direct reference to the experimental conditions, we have in sensate experience to do with separate observations whose correlation can only be indicated by their belonging to the wholeness of mind.

It is our endeavor to show that man has reached a turning point in consciousness, that his relationship with his creative self demands a clarification that can widen and deepen his understanding of the nature of reality. Work is made for man, not man for work. This Series hopes to demonstrate the sacramental character of work which is more easily achieved when the principal objects of our attention have taken on a symbolic form that is generally recognized and accepted: in other words, when there is an established iconography relating to the meaningful interpretation of man and his vocation. This suggests a "law" in the relationship of a person and his chosen discipline: that it is valuable only when the spiritual, the creative, life is strong enough to insist on some expression through symbols. For no work can be based on material, technological or physical aspirations alone.

The human race is now entering upon a new phase of evolutionary progress, a phase in which, impelled by the forces of evolution itself, it must converge upon itself and convert itself into one single human organism dominated by a reconciliation of knowing and being in their inner unity and destined to make a qualitative leap into a higher form of consciousness that would transcend and complement individual consciousness as we know it, or otherwise destroy itself. For the entire universe is one vast field, potential for incarnation, and achieving incandescence here and there of reason and spirit. What to some is mystery and inscrutability, to others symbolizes and declares the very nature of the cosmic process. And in the whole world of *quality* with which category by the nature of our minds we necessarily make contact, we here and there apprehend pre-eminent value. This can be achieved only if we recognize that we are unable to focus our attention on the particulars of a whole without diminishing our comprehension of the whole, and of course conversely, we can focus on the whole only by diminishing our comprehension of the particulars which constitute the whole.

This Series is designed to present a kind of intellectual autobiography of each author, to portray the nature and meaning of the creative process for the creator and to show the relevance of his work to the feelings and aspirations of the man of flesh and bone. This Series endeavors to reflect also the influence of the work on the man and on society and to point to the freedom, or lack of freedom, to choose and pursue one profession rather than another. It attempts to emphasize that the creator in any realm must surrender himself to a passionate pursuit of the hidden meaning of his labors, guided by deep personal intimations of an as yet undiscovered reality.

These volumes endeavor to indicate that it is impossible to know what constitutes a good society unless we know what defines a good individual. The self is determined by the values according to which it subordinates and integrates the rest of its values. If the values be transient, so is the self. If the values be dispersed and incoherent, so is the self. If they are organic and integrated, so is the self. The unity of human personality is its soundness. The unified self cannot be understood in terms of its constituent parts as dissected away from each other. So that finally what we see and what we do are no more and no less than what we are.

It is the effort of *The Credo Series* to define the new reality in which the estrangement of man and his work, resulting in the self-estrangement in man's existence, is overcome. This new reality is born through the reconciliation of what a man *knows* with what a man *is*. Being itself in all its presuppositions and implications can only be understood through the totality, through wholeness. St. Paul, who, like Isaiah before him, went into the market place not to secularize truth but to proclaim it, taught man that the "new creation" could be explained only by conquering the daemonic cleavages, the destructive split, in soul and cosmos; and that fragmentation always destroys a unity, produces a tearing away from the source and thereby creates disunity and isolation. The fruit can never be separated from the tree. The Tree of Life can never be disjoined from the Tree of Knowledge for both have *one and the same* root. And if man allows himself to fall into isolation, if he seeks to maintain a self segregated from the totality of which he is a necessary part, if he chooses to remain asunder, unrelated to the original context of all created things in which he too has his place—including his own labors—then this act of apostasy bears fruit in the demiurgical presumption of *magic,* a form of animism in which man seeks an authority of the self, placing himself above the law of the universe by attempting to separate the inseparable. He thus creates an unreal world of false contexts after having destroyed or deserted the real. And in this way the method of analysis, of scientific objectivity, which is good and necessary in its right place, is endowed with a destructive power when it is allowed to usurp a place for which it is not fitted.

The naturalist principle that man is the measure of all things has been shattered more than ever in our own age by the question, "What is the measure of man?" Postmodern man is more profoundly perplexed about the nature of man than his ancestors were. He is on the verge of spiritual and moral insanity. He does not know who he is. And having lost the sense of who and what he is, he fails to grasp the meaning of his fellow man, of his vocation and of the nature and purpose of knowledge itself. For what is not understood cannot be known. And it is this cognitive faculty which is frequently abrogated by the "scientific" theory of knowledge, a theory that refuses to recognize the existence of comprehensive entities as distinct from their particulars. The central act of knowing is indeed that form of comprehension which is never absent from any process of knowing and is finally its ultimate sanction.

Science itself acknowledges as real a host of entities that cannot be described completely in materialistic or mechanistic terms, and it is this transcendence out of the domain of science into a region from which science itself can be appraised that *The Credo Series* hopes to expose. For the essence of the ebb and flow of experience, of sensations, the richness of the immediacy of directly apprehended knowledge, the metaphysical substance of what assails our being, is the very act itself of sensation and affection and therefore must escape the net of rational analysis, yet is intimately related to every cognitive act. It is this increasing intellectual climate that is calling into birth once more the compelling Socratic questions, "What is the purpose of life, the meaning of work?" "What is man?" Plato himself could give us only an indirect answer: "Man is declared to be that creature who is constantly in search of himself, a creature who at every moment of his existence must examine and scrutinize the conditions of his existence. He is a being in search of meaning."

Theory and life always go together. An organic conception of man and his work, man and society, man and the universe, is portrayed in First Corinthians 12 when Paul relates the famous story of the strife that once broke out between the parts of the human body. They refused to fulfill their special functions within the organism until they finally learned that they are all parts of one body and can exist and function only as such. For they all breathe together. And by so doing subordinate themselves to the presentation of the whole body. What may be an explanation of organic life in the human body may be transferred to the life in the universe and to the relationship between the interior and the exterior, for all is permeated by the life-giving creative power—by unity.

The authors in this endeavor are aware that man in the twentieth century finds himself in the greatest revolution since the discovery of agriculture. They show, each in his own way, that part of the meaning of our present turmoil may indeed lie in its being the means to reconcile thought and action, to overcome the parochialism of dogmas that only isolate man from man and man from the implicit meaning of his chosen profession. Our effort is to create an image of man intelligible and unitary, a microcosmic mirror of the greater macrocosm of which he is a part and in which he has his legitimate place in relation to the whole. For even the extraordinary successes of scientific predictions, the fruits of man's ingenuity in inventing the scientific method, seem comprehensible only on the basis that the human mind possesses an inherent logic closely parallel with the structure of the external world itself.

The very interdependence of the observer and the participant can no longer be ignored as part of the essential value of things. To take a definitive example from modern cosmology, it is challenging indeed to note that there is a most unusual connection between the existence of stars and the laws that govern the atomic nuclei. Emphasis is placed upon the existence, not the properties, of stars. For everyone expects the properties of stars and atomic nuclei to be related. It is the *connection* with the *existence* of stars that is so reassuring—and indeed surprising.

From this it is evident that there is present in the universe a *law* applicable to all nature including man and his work. Life itself then is seen to be a creative process elaborating and maintaining *order* out of the randomness of matter, endlessly generating new and unexpected structures and properties by building up associations that qualitatively transcend their constituent parts. This is not to diminish the importance of "scientific objectivity." It is, however, to say that the mind possesses a quality that cannot be isolated or known exclusively in the sense of objective knowledge. For it consists in that elusive humanity in us, our self, that knows. It is that inarticulate awareness that includes and *comprehends* all we know. It consists in the irreducible active voice of man and is recognized only in other things, only when the circle of consciousness closes around its universe of events.

The experience of the modern mind has been expressed in terms of conflict produced by false dualisms, disruption, self-destruction, meaninglessness, purposelessness and desperation. This character of our time has found its expression in literature, in art, in existential philosophy, in some forms of natural science, in political demonologies, and is explored in the psychology of the unconscious. Our authors hope to indicate that through a quickening of awareness man can overcome this dualism and can rise to face the meaning of life and work, keeping his mind and energies awake at full stretch. Such knowledge—that form of knowledge which cannot be disjoined from being—will enable man to embrace life with passion and to work with devotion. It will enable him to absorb experience with his whole nature and thereby to fill a want that is satisfied neither by action alone nor by thought alone. This unity of *being* and *doing* has a justifiable claim to be called a form of enchantment since through it men, who might otherwise give in to the malice of circumstances and conditions, find their old powers revived or new powers stirring within them, and through these life is sustained, renewed and fulfilled.

Man is now confronting himself with the compelling need to create an organic identification between what he *is* and what he *does*. For only in this way can the threat of conformism and the treachery of abstraction, the plight of the modern mind, be conquered. This split, inherited from the seventeenth century, between the transitive and the intransitive, between the creator and the process of creativity, has blunted man's appetite for experience. Language itself in our time has failed because man has forgotten that it is the mother of thought, because of its analytical emphasis, and thus lacks ready means to convey associations, emotional or imaginative, that cluster around a subject and give to it a distinctive personal significance. In other words, the symbols by which man lives and has his being, that "tacit coefficient" * of articulate knowledge that is unanalyzable, now knocks at the portals of consciousness waiting to be admitted. For human nature loses its most precious quality when it is robbed of its sense of things beyond, unexplored and yet insistent.

The Credo Series belongs to those ideas that are intuitively conceived and that originate in spheres of a spiritual order and surprise thought, as it were, compelling it to transform its inherited notions conformably with its en-

---

* See the classical work, *Personal Knowledge,* by Michael Polanyi for an enlarged meaning of the nature of reality. (University of Chicago Press, 1958.)

larged vision of the nature of things. It is as though the
authors of the Series were recovering this reality out of a
memory of a lost harmony, a memory latent in the soul
and not distilled from the changing things of mere physical
observation. In this way the inner unity of the known and
the knower may be preserved, and the almost mythic in-
tuition of reality thereby related to its conceptual and
rational forms of expression. For man, unlike a machine,
is an organism existing as an end in itself. He *is* the system on which causal explanations are based and to which
they have to return; he *is* a historically existent whole, a
four-dimensional entity, and not merely an abstraction
from which statements about phenomena are deducible
under the guise of eternity.

Our hope is to point to a new dimension of morality—
not that of constraint and prohibition but a morality that
lies as a fountainhead within the human soul, a morality
of aspiration to spiritual experience. It suggests that necessity is laid upon us to infer entities that are not observed
and are not observable. For an unseen universe is necessary to explain the seen. The flux is seen, but to account
for its structure and its nature we infer particles of various
kinds to serve as the vertices of the changing patterns,
placing less emphasis on the isolated units and more on
the structure and nature of relations. The process of
knowing involves an immaterial becoming, an immaterial
identification, and finally, knowledge itself is seen to be
a dependent variable of immateriality. And somewhere
along this spiritual pilgrimage man's pure observation is
relinquished and gives way to the deeper experience of
awe, for there can be no explanation of a phenomenon by

searching for its origin but only by discerning its immanent law—this quality of transcendence that abides even in matter itself.

The present situation in the world and the vast accretion of knowledge have produced a serious anxiety, which may be overcome by re-evaluating the character, kinship, logic and operation of man in relation to his work. For work implies goals and intimately affects the person performing the work. Therefore the correlation and relatedness of ideas, facts and values that are in perpetual interplay could emerge from these volumes as they point to the inner synthesis and organic unity of man and his labors. For though no labor alone can enrich the person, no enrichment can be achieved without absorbing and intense labor. We then experience a unity of faith, labor and grace which prepares the mind for receiving a truth from sources over which it has no control. This is especially true since the great challenge of our age arises out of man's inventions in relation to his life.

Thus *The Credo Series* seeks to encourage the perfection not only of man's works but also and above all the fulfillment of himself as a person. And so we now are summoned to consider not only man in the process of development as a human subject but also his influence on the object of his investigation and creation. Observation alone is interference. The naïve view that we can observe any system and predict its behavior without altering it by the very act of observation was an unjustified extrapolation from Newton's *Celestial Mechanics*. We can observe the moon or even a satellite and predict its behavior without appreciably interfering with it, but we cannot do this with an amoeba, far less with a man and still less with a society of men. It is the heart of the question of the nature of work itself. If we regard our labors as a process of shaping or forming, then the fruits of our labors play the part of a mold by which we ourselves are shaped. And this means, in the preservation of the identity of the knower and the known, that cognition and generation, that is, creation, though in different spheres, are nevertheless alike.

It is hoped that the influence of such a Series may help to overcome the serious bifurcation of function and meaning and may show that the extraordinary crisis through which the world is passing can be fruitfully met by recognizing that knowledge has not been completely dehumanized and has not totally degenerated into a mere notebook over-crowded with formulas that few are able to understand or apply.

For mankind is now engaged in composing a new theme. Life refuses to be embalmed alive. Life cannot abjure life; nothing that lives is born out of nothingness. But nothing, either, can preserve its form against the ceaseless flux of being. Life never manifests itself in negative terms. And our hope lies in drawing from every category of work a conviction that non-material values can be discovered in positive, affirmative, visible things. The estrangement between the temporal and non-temporal man is coming to an end, community is inviting communion and a vision of the human condition more worthy of man is engendered, connecting ever more closely the creative mind with the currents of spiritual energy which breaks for us the bonds of habit and keeps us in touch with the permanence of being in all its fullness through our work.

And as, long ago, the Bearers of Bread were succeeded by the Bearers of Torches, so now, in the immediacies of life, it is the image of man and his vocation that can re-kindle the high passion of humanity in its quest for light. Refusing to divorce work from life or love from knowl-edge, it is action, it is passion that enhances our being.

We live in an expanding universe and also in the moral infinite of that other universe, the universe of man. And along the whole stretched arc of this universe we may see that extreme limit of complicity where reality seems to shape itself within the work man has chosen for his realiza-tion. Work then becomes not only a way of knowledge, it becomes even more a way of life—of life in its totality. For the last end of every maker is himself.

"And the places that have been desolate for ages shall be built in thee: thou shalt raise up the foundations of generation and generation; and thou shalt be called the repairer of the fences, turning the paths into rest." *

—RUTH NANDA ANSHEN

* Isaiah, 58:12

INTRODUCTION

Queen: Do not for ever with thy vailèd lids
          Seek for thy noble father in the dust.
          Thou know'st 'tis common; all that lives must die,
          Passing through nature to eternity.
Hamlet: Ay, madam, it is common.
Queen: If it be,
          Why seems it so particular with thee?
Hamlet: Seems, madam! Nay, it is. I know not "seems."

Perhaps the foregoing is one of the earliest recorded dialogues between the deductive, categorizing rationalist and the existentialist. The facile, unfeeling classifying of his grief by his mother does not satisfy the young prince; he does not feel his father's death as a "passing through nature to eternity." It is particular, and, more important, it *is*. This awareness is the starting point of his thought and action for the remainder of his life.

For Pope Paul, also, the human condition is particular, and *is*. Man in the world is the focus of his interest—man in the context of the material, of which he is, in great part, creator and lord. The instrument of this creation, human work, at once enriching and corrupting, is the fulcrum of the tension that is the chief characteristic of the life of modern man, torn as he is between the simultaneous pulls of matter and spirit. Thus the thought of Pope Paul over a period of thirty years has centered in man as responsible actor, however frightened, enslaved and self-destructive he may be. For man, he assumes implicitly and naturally the freedom that is the legacy of Christ, disturbing but divinizing for Everyman who is to exercise it.

Pope Paul's message is therefore to transform and transcend, with transcendence itself becoming the existentialist, propulsive force of human life. He believes that the energy of transcendence must be generated within man himself; but that transcendence is accomplished in the manner spoken of by Teilhard de Chardin: through multiple contacts with the world, "the Christian pre-adheres to God."

The Pope's dialogue with the world of Everyman, "with the profound voices of the modern world" promised in his coronation speech, is a continuation of a dialogue begun many years before. It is not merely verbal; it has been maintained through his years in the Vatican Secretariat of State, and the Archbishopric of Milan; now as the Bishop of Rome and Successor to Peter he continues to reveal a surprisingly imaginative perspective on the significant affairs and fortunes of the modern world.

One who undertakes to follow the thought of the man who is Pope Paul VI notes first that he has done more than the usual amount of writing and speaking in his forty-three years as a priest. His language is seen to be at once profuse and direct, expressed with a personal freshness and authenticity which his office might tend sometimes to obscure. His habit of wide reading has kept his thought and opinion in constant flow toward articulation, even when opportunity for expression may have been wanting. His judgments concerning the world, both favorable and adverse, are not the expression of a remote observation of the affairs of men; nor are they drawn from the burdens and vicissitudes of penitents exclusively or from the often misinterpreted and unreflective reportage of the events in daily news journals. Much of the present Pope's knowledge of the situation of mankind has come to him through pastoral experience. But in addition a wide-ranging literary experience has helped shape a natural sensitivity for the less obvious and a surprisingly unclerical aversion for the categorical. Paul VI has a reflective, analytical mind. To explore these characteristics of the personality of the man who has now become the official spokesman of Christendom is to be brought face to face with the fine web of his integrity, and with the restlessness of a mind constantly concerned with the tensions and crises of man's temporal struggle.

The announcement early in his pontificate that he would continue Pope John's dialogue, reassuring though it was to the entire world, was, in a sense, unnecessary. The substance of his pastoral letters and discourses as Archbishop of Milan refers regularly to the world at its widest and most diverse. Concern for the psychic welfare of man, which is the very condition of his religious and social orientation, finds its way into much of Pope Paul's writing. Directly and indirectly he reiterates the belief that man can turn fully to God only after he has made a thorough assessment of himself and the goods of this world. He sees human experience as the focal point of man's life, and seems himself haunted by the prospect of barrenness and silence to be encountered by the man whose estimation of life is materialistic. In his letters, especially, he reminds men that the formal elements of life must themselves be charged with vitality, must be turned into experience, if man is not to be enslaved and paralyzed. In this reference he includes the formal elements of work and worship, and no man, however deprived of learning and the advantages of higher cultural resources, is considered to be insensible to this appeal for personal revitalization.

The social sense of Paul VI is a combination of the idealistic and practical. His counsels and recommendations on poverty, for example, stressing its personal advantages, its worth in itself as the very fastness of detachment and spiritual equilibrium, should not be summarily judged as an attempt to cool man's indignation at social inequality. Such a simplistic interpretation would put the reader at a great disadvantage in knowing the mind of Pope Paul. By reference and by act he has stressed the dignity of the forgotten individual, the economic zero, and has urged the more fortunate to take upon themselves the raising of the level of human life. It should be remembered that many of his words on poverty are in the tradition of pastoral and homiletic literature; and it is not a tradition that has directed the pastor to the exploration of all sides of a question. Though the present Pope may be in advance of this tradition in psychological penetration and, occasionally, in social implication, in the dialectic of his pastoral writing, he is strictly orthodox.

Characteristic, also, of his thought is his susceptibility, in spite of an occasionally hostile judgment, to the "modern mind," the modern writer, and even to the prophets of the absurd. Modern man himself, he says, is a prophet of the absurd. "It is he who derides himself." It is often possible to detect in his words a compassion and imaginative understanding of absurdity, though not intellectual agreement. He is seldom seen to be without sympathy for the attitude that expresses fury at the meaninglessness of the universe, and that finds some solace in the extrarational excursion into the flux of man's own bodily and psychic life.

His sympathetic reference to Dostoevski's treatment of sin and the nonviability of remorse (though essentially a rejection of Dostoevski's own *via*), his criticism of Sartre's and Camus' reliance on the reasonable to present the absurd, his pointing to Greek tragedy's preoccupation with sin and suffering—these show not merely a feeling for literature, but, what is more rare and significant, a sense of the necessary relationship between literature, theology and religion. Although his alacrity in dismissing the burden or "statement" of many of these works may prove irritating, it should be remembered that he speaks pastorally, directed by a vision that is creative in its own right, "straitened" to use all things to serve itself.

The indefinability of faith, the urgency of action, the pressure of history, the *donnée* in man's life, his encounter with himself and the world—these are the core of his thinking, not consideration of "types" of men, not speculation on individual and separate "faculties." Jean Danielou's important point, that the stumbling block to the man seeking God is man's universe of man-created things, is a repeated theme. It seems to have shaped Pope Paul's interest in the workingman as much as the often-discussed "apostasy of the working classes." He gives it varied forms, shadings and applications.

Where scholastic philosophy has not defined traditional

terms for him, he displays a personal disregard for the
univocal. His definition of the term "the world," for example, as "life lived outside the light," the "result of ideas
which are approximative, of comfortable opinions . . .
the way born of comfort and not of duty," presents no
easy dichotomy between good and evil, no double gateway
clearly marked with warning for the Christian. His explanations indicate the ability to see that many modern
Christians yield to the world without either renouncing
or examining the formalities of their Christianity. In contemporary life Christianity takes on a social and cultural
context which is often identified with the spiritual; in the
minds and lives of many Christians, indeed, this context
is frequently substituted for the spiritual life, which the
term "Christian" implicitly presupposes. Paul sees also
that the accentuated diversity of modern life makes double thinking convenient and attractive. Yet he seldom invites complacency by an oversimplification. He speaks
of characteristics of the world's present moral crisis in
terms that reflect a sensitivity to both its obvious and
subtle elements. It is "a resistance toward authority," but
also "a dislike of what is easy, seemingly providential,
and facile of solution."

There is no attempt here to claim for the Pope a greater
complexity than he possesses, nor to disclaim for him the
simplicity of approach which is all too characteristic of
religious writers, and certainly exaggerated in some of
them. The Catholic thinker necessarily speaks on many
subjects in terms that seem to reflect a starkly simple system of thought. Starting as he does with the simplicity of
God, he sees the foundations of his universe in this light,
and advances valid arguments to substantiate the meta-

physical truth of his position. Often, a skeptical mind objects to the position of certitude only because it is uncomplex. When, for instance, the Pope urges the scientist to look beyond matter itself to find the harmony of the physical order, he may seem sanguine to some men of science. And yet many intellectuals of the world would urge the same search—if not to find harmony, then to find meaning. Some intellectual and moral stances must be delineated in an utterly lucid idiom, since they represent theistic and religious positions born of a faith that itself is simple, because it is direct and prior to all else. An unswerving belief in the absolute, while it can reduce even the psychological and the historical dimension to an unwarranted homogeneity, must lead its professors to assertions of direct clarity in the basic areas of human thought.

In these pages, the modern stress on the psychological and historical at the expense of the moral and eschatological receives but glancing attention in some questions which would ordinarily claim such stress. Pope Paul's pastoral letter on marriage, which analyzes the purposes of the married state and the conditions for its stability, will encourage the moralist and the Christian student of society rather than the more psychologically oriented. In his remarks on art also, and in certain scattered references to literature, his historical and esthetic consciousness is thrown into shadow by the judgment of the moralist or liturgist.

It is interesting, however, to note that in his studies of the religious and moral sense, the Church, the priesthood, ecumenism, there is present the very psychological and historical insight that is less incisive elsewhere. He is impressed, but not deceived, by the virtual disappearance of

avarice from modern life, where material goods and money
are so generally abundant that they inspire unconscious
dependence, rather than passion. "Sin," he says, "reverberates in God." "If we take away the sense of sin from life,
we drain it of its dramatic value." The implication of this
observation for an understanding of modern literature represents one of those flashes of insight on the part of Paul
that cause one to long for the modern humanist Pope, who
would draw upon the theater for example to show con-
cretely what befalls man when he can no longer sin, but
only "err"; what befalls when he sees himself in a morass
from which he finds no escape.

The total perspective of his thought embraces most of
the sources of anxiety in the contemporary world. His
counsels on peace have a special urgency, since they reveal a personal horror of the catastrophic possibilities of
nuclear war. It is in preponderantly general terms that he
speaks on human justice, leaving to individual countries
its specific application. He is concerned with human progress in science, social relations, and education; with the
fact that the new scientific and technological achievements
can add to our knowledge of God, and to the idiom with
which we praise him. These and any other bonds uniting
men in common effort toward the well-being of all he
subjects to reflection, and speaks of with a sense of his
own involvement.

This book attempts to construct a sequence of Pope
Paul's reflections on specific subjects, culled from the
speeches and writings of a lifetime, rather than to record
discourses in their entirety, or, on the other hand, to present epigrams and *sententiae*. And to counteract the automatic impression of the impersonality of office or the

symbol of authority usually created by a Pope's words, the first person singular has been used wherever the pontifical "we" would ordinarily be indicated. It is hoped that this form may present Pope Paul VI as less pontificating than pondering; as more discursive than aphoristic.

The English translation of the Pope's words as well as the arrangement of the text have been carried out by myself.

A synthesis of the lifelong response that Pope Paul has made to his world, emerges of its own power from the pages that follow. It is a true Credo, whose multiple elements will find continuing expansion and elaboration in the years which remain to his pontificate.

JOHN G. CLANCY

St. John's University
New York

I

CREDO

By his birth and training the Pope necessarily belongs to one country and to a particular civilization and culture. The high office which he fills gives universal dimensions to his heart and mind. Thus, in this moment of encounter, I would wish to speak all your languages, and be able to say, in the idiom and forms most familiar to you, a word of greeting, of respect and of profound cordiality. Even as the Church, I am the enemy of no one and I know no other language than that of friendship and trust.[1]

God has entrusted this Church to me not only that I may preserve it in its holiness and in the richness of its vigor, but also, as Christ himself has commanded, that I may devote to it my thoughts, my care, and even, if need be, my life itself. I will work so that its power, its light, and its riches, which are altogether divine and infinite, may be poured out upon men ever more widely.[2]

It is to the city of Rome and to the world that my divine mandate is now spread. But it is precisely because I have been raised to the summit of the Church's hierarchy that I feel as though I have been placed in the lowest office as servant of the servants of God.[2]

The authority and responsibility of this office are marvelously joined, the dignity with the humility, the rights with the duties, the power with the love.[2]

He who has indicated His will through the consent of my venerable brothers, the Fathers of the College of Cardinals, has entrusted to me the care and the responsibility of the holy Church. He will know how to give my heart, fearful at the vastness of the task imposed, a watchful and serene strength, a tireless zeal for His glory, and a missionary concern for the spread of the Gospel throughout the world in charity and love.[3]

I will not forget the admonition of Christ whose vicar I have become: "Let him who is greatest among you become as the youngest, and he who is the chief as the servant." [3]

We are all responsible for the time in which we live, for the life of our brothers, and we are responsible before our Christian conscience. We are responsible before Christ, before the Church, before the judgment of history, responsible in the very presence of God.[4]

Therefore I am conscious in this moment of taking a pledge, sacred, solemn and most serious: that of continuing in time and spreading on earth the mission of Christ.[2]

I take this pledge before the history of the Church of the past, derived with vital integrity from the Lord Jesus.[2]

I take this pledge before the Church of the future, which expects only that I show fidelity to the first preaching of the Gospel and to the authentic tradition which sprang from it.[2]

I take this pledge before the history of the Church of today which I know and which I will study in order to know even better its structure, its life, its richness and its needs.[2]

The law of God ties us to itself, not to the past, and it obligates us to new ventures which we would wish were even better than those of the past. Out of its own perfection there arises from the law that hunger and thirst for justice that every Christian should feel.[5]

At the beginning of my ministry, remembrance of my predecessors, who have bequeathed to me a sacred and glorious spiritual heritage, comes spontaneously and joyously to mind: Pius XI, with his toughness of soul; Pius XII, who illumined the Church with the light of a teaching full of wisdom; and finally John XXIII, who gave the whole world the example of his unique goodness.[3]

In a very special way, and with grateful remembrance, I recall the person of John XXIII who, in a brief but intense ministry, was able to win over to himself the hearts of men, even those distant and estranged. He did so by an unceasing solicitude, a sincere and concrete goodness toward the lowly of this earth, and by the pastoral character of his activity. And to these qualities was added the individual charm of the human gifts of his great heart.[3]

The light that shone forth from his person upon souls deepened in intensity like a burning flame, until the moment of the final sacrifice of himself, endured with a strength of soul that convulsed the world, gathering all mankind around his bed of pain and giving them "one heart and one soul" in a single outburst of reverence, veneration and prayer.[3]

One of the tasks of any Pope to which my predecessor gave such unforgettable witness is to contribute to the affirmation of peace. As he so authoritatively reminded us, such peace must rest on the four pillars of truth, justice, love, and liberty. Following his example I intend to do everything I can in this direction.[6]

The Master has wished to place a crushing weight on my poor shoulders. Perhaps it is because they are the weakest, and the best suited to show that it is not He who needs anything from me. It may be that acting through the frailest of His children, He wishes to pour forth in presence and in love a witness to His infinite power and good pleasure, to His mercy which is beyond the telling.[7]

Thus something marvelous has happened in my life: Simon is transformed into Peter. Simon, the disciple full of heart and fire, changeable, excitable, weak and fragile, becomes Peter according to the name that the Lord has given him, by the special grace poured out on him, and with the responsibility of the keys of the kingdom entrusted to him. It is a change that allows Simon under many aspects to continue to be Simon.[7]

In applying this Gospel excerpt to myself, I want to say that whatever there is that is sacred and good and human in what binds me to you—this will remain.[7]

What will happen to me? I do not know. The Lord keeps hidden from our eyes the message of the future. He Himself did this to Peter. Jesus said to the Prince of the Apostles: "Another will lead thee." You will be overwhelmed by duty, by obligations, by situations that will make you suffer and demand finally the offering of your life. The prediction that Christ made to Peter was a prediction of witness and of martyrdom, a presage of pain and of blood.[7]

One thing I assure you. On that day—and it could be every day of my life—in which I find myself tired and overcome to the point of feeling myself like the old Simon, weak, vacillating, and full of insufficiency, I will think that you are close to me with your prayers, with your charity and with your love. I will think that you wish me no longer to be Simon but Peter—quick not only to strengthen my own faith and my own incorruptible commitment to the Lord Jesus, but to confirm it and strengthen it in you and in all the brethren.[7]

The extent of the task that awaits my feeble strength is such as to dismay the humble priest summoned to this high office. But daily I shall devote my prayers and my efforts to it. There is need, however, of your collaboration and of your prayers, rising incessantly to God for the pastor of the universal Church. It is for this reason that my grateful thoughts turn to all the children of the Catholic Church who give the world the witness of their faith, the vision of their union, and the royal splendor of their dignity.[3]

At this time when all mankind is looking toward this throne of truth and toward the man who has been called to represent the Divine Saviour here on earth, I can only renew my appeal for an understanding that is loyal, open, full of good will, and able to unite men in sincere respect for each other. I call for every effort that can be made to save humanity, to favor the peaceful development of the rights God has given it, and to facilitate its spiritual and religious life, so that it may be brought to a more lively and heartfelt worship of its Creator.[3]

There is no lack of encouraging signs reaching me

from men of good will. I thank God for these, while I offer everyone my quiet but resolute cooperation for the maintenance of the great gift of peace in the world.[3]

I embrace with a father's love all those who suffer: those who are ill, those who are poor, those who are in prison, those who are in exile, those who are refugees.[3]

I greet all my children in Christ, among whom especially I delight to mention the young, full of courage and generosity, in whom is founded the sure hope of a better future. I greet the innocence of childhood; the humble and the great of the earth; all the craftsmen and workers whose toil I know and appreciate so well; those who devote themselves to the arts and to study, to teaching and to science; journalists and publicists; politicians and heads of state.[3]

May each in his particular vocation and responsibility make his contribution to the building of an order that grows more just in its principles, more effective in the application of its laws, more healthy in its private and public morals, ever more willing to defend the peace.[3]

My words are for those, who, without belonging to the Catholic Church, are united to us by the powerful bond of faith and love of Jesus Christ, and marked with the unique seal of baptism—one Lord, one faith, one baptism. I speak out of an immense desire, the same that has moved so many among them, to hasten the blessed day that will see, after so many centuries of unhappy separation, the realization of Christ's prayer on the eve of His death— *ut unum sint,* that they may be one.[2]

Beyond the frontiers of Christianity, there is another dialogue in which the Church is engaged today—the dialogue with the modern world. A superficial examination of the man of today reveals him to be more and more a stranger to all that is religious and spiritual. Aware of the progress of science and technology, intoxicated by spectacular successes in domains until now unexplored, he seems to consider his own powers divine and to wish to take the place of God.[2]

Behind the world's façade I hear these profound voices of the modern world. It is a world obsessed also with a desire for things of the spirit and of grace. It is a world that aspires to justice and to a progress not merely technical, but deeply human. And finally, it is a world that seeks a peace that goes beyond the mere suspension of hostilities and offers a possibility of development and collaboration between all nations in an atmosphere of mutual trust and confidence.[2]

I will listen to these voices of the world. With the aid of God and the example of my predecessors I will continue untiringly to offer humanity the remedy for its ills, the answer to its pleadings: *investigabiles divitias Christi,* Christ and his unfathomable riches. Will my voice be heard? [2]

THE WORLD VIEWS CHRISTIANITY:

MAN AND HIS TEMPORAL DIMENSION

The Human Predicament

II

THE MODERN MIND

THE VAST PANORAMA of the modern world lies before us, its life vibrating with thought, activity, and achievement. The city of man is in a process of unceasing change. New forms of civilization continue to evolve on a scale never before seen.[8]

Man himself is increasing in numbers, in knowledge, and in power. Research, business, new ventures and interests, diversions, and amusements—these are the stuff of his dreams and his plans for the future. His mind is absorbed in his work, his social commitments and in the pursuit of pleasure. Whatever is immediate and real holds him enthralled, and even his highest hopes have no aspiration beyond the present life.[8]

The earth is his kingdom.[8]

Life is in full transformation. A new civilization is rising out of the marvelous employment of riches and forces of nature. The forms of life have become so modified that even customs, social relations and political expressions must of necessity also undergo change.[5]

A major consequence of modern life is that men's minds have become engrossed in the conquest of the world around them. Modern man is interested in phenomena

rather than in substance, in appearance rather than reality, in the visible rather than the invisible, matter rather
than spirit, the present rather than the past or future,
earth rather than heaven, the useful rather than the good,
diversion rather than duty, the here rather than the here-
after, man rather than God.[8]

While man's conquest of the world of nature is not in
itself an evil, it is in practice a kind of hindrance to his
spiritual development. The world of nature, as such, is
exactly suited to man's intellectual capacity and this is of
unbounded interest to him. Today, however, a vast number of minds are absorbed in it almost to the exclusion of
everything else.[8]

It is from an intense study of matter, riddled with secrets
and rich in energy, that science has been born.[8]

The certainty that scientific knowledge achieves ban-
ishes every other kind of certainty from men's minds as
being either without foundation or a form of superstition.
Science enlists the energy of man, and it is this that has
tamed nature and turned it to man's advantage. Technology adds a further refinement by turning things into
instruments for man's own ends. Thus the distraction of
utility adds to the delusion of spiritual uncertainty.[8]

And so the art of producing *things* has triumphed. Industry and commerce have surrounded modern man with
such an abundance of sophisticated riches that he is constantly bemused by the heady illusion of complete happiness. He is tempted to believe that the whole circle of
objective reality, which is his environmental world, and
the realm of subjective satisfaction, which is that of his
spirit, can be summed up in this wonderful, exhilarating
and transitory experience.[8]

And so man has become a prisoner in his own vast, materialistic cage.[8]

The contemplative life has been almost abandoned: modern society lacks men of silence, of solitude, men rich in interior life, to guide and accompany it on its precarious human way toward its final destiny.[8]

Yet man believes that he has acquired happiness. This easy and proud illusion has been born in him by the study that he has dedicated to knowledge and to the domination of the natural world; by the labor he has endured to transform it and render it useful, and the immense riches that have poured forth from it. His interests, centered in facts and goods that are economic and utilitarian by nature, have fed it.[9]

Even if he does not yet believe that he has found contentment, he is convinced that it lies along this route, and that therefore this is the road to follow. All of life is viewed as being centered in economic gain, on which the personal and social efficiency of man is made to depend.[9]

This is the materialistic view of life, with its enormous moral repercussions.[9]

And thus we are brought full circle to face once more historical materialism. Here again are its simplistic ways, its incapacity to understand the complex reality of the universe, its ability to torment man by using the stimuli of his hunger and his hope of justice, measured only by the temporal and economic order. And here too are its spiritual insensitivity and its inability to understand religious values, its final denial of God.[9]

The study of moral obligation, divorced from divine

law and sanction, loses all urgency and meaning. Sin no longer exists. And to uphold this chilling principle, which can be only a source of moral anarchy, all genuine remorse, all repentance that might lead man back to God is stifled at birth. Man's moral and religious senses stand or fall together, and moral crisis becomes in the end a crisis of faith.[8]

Liberty is no longer regarded as freedom to choose what is right but as license to do what one pleases, and it has become its own end.[8]

Two things characterize human activity today: first, the attempt to free it from anything that lies beyond human law, emptied of any natural and absolute foundation; second, the attempt to free it from anything that is beyond human consciousness reduced to the narcissistic level of psychological analysis.[8]

Modern man has almost wholly neglected the study of "being" in itself, and of the human soul. He has confined himself to external phenomena and psychological experiences. He no longer concerns himself with his transcendent but innate capacity to reach out to something beyond the pale of natural experience. No longer does he feel the quickening urge to go beyond the frontiers of the finite world.[8]

From his concern with the study of well-being, he moves on to the study of consciousness, and he comes to regard himself as the unique master of his own mind. How he can do this in the light of reason and his own practical experience is difficult to see; indeed, sooner or later it becomes a clear absurdity.[8]

But, given such premises, the conclusion is logical: the worship of man is taking the place of the worship of God.

In order to extinguish this desire for God, it has been necessary to blindfold man. It has been necessary to deprive him of the power of seeing what lies outside himself and the world of sense, without his recognizing that through this fatal blindness people and things lose first their significance and then their value.[8]

And this is what lies behind all the tragedies—spiritual, cultural, social, and political—in the world of today as it spins on its giddy course, emptied of its basic core of security, order and peace.[8]

I fully understand the attitude of those whose thinking has been penetrated by this experience so typical of our times. Some of them are ill at ease in the blind negation of obsolete scientism. Others are disturbed. Still others are apathetic, hostile, or almost resigned to the conclusion that life lacks direction and purpose.[10]

Among thoughtful people, many are worried by the decay of that religious consciousness which is at the root of the most solid and the most valuable achievements of the human spirit.[10]

"What," they ask, "what of the Kingdom of Heaven? The future life? Man's supernatural destiny? The mystery of life and of the universe? And God?"[8]

Modern man is in the process of losing his religious sense.[8]

The religious sense is a natural human aptitude to perceive that we have some relationship to God.[8]

It is religion's subjective basis, without which it either remains a formalistic, external, feeble and unproductive thing, or else collapses altogether. This is the special danger today.[8]

We call it religious feeling when it becomes active and

aware of its own perceptions. It is worth noting, however, that today in ordinary speech the two expressions "religious sense" and "religious feeling" are often used interchangeably.[8]

Under the expression "religious sense" are included the multiple and complex manifestations of man's general tendency toward God. In a sense it precedes human reasoning, but it derives its *raison d'être* from reality.[8]

When the religious sense thus understood receives the divine word, this reception engages not only the mind but also the other faculties, and introduces into the relationship a new factor of prime importance which we call the heart. Then the religious sense becomes an awareness of presence and communion, a purely religious thing, so that the divine word is not simply accepted passively but calls forth from us a warm and vital response.[8]

The religious sense is not equally active and developed in all human beings. In terms of natural endowment, some people have a naturally quick and sensitive religious perception like an ear for music. In others it is slower and duller. There are differences, too, in people's cultivation or neglect of this spiritual gift. Children, the pure in heart, the spiritually alert, the wise, the mystics, all in their varied ways possess this wonderful aptitude to an exceptional degree.[8]

If a man seeks and listens for the word of God, the truth that brings life and salvation enters his soul and creates a new bond between him and God; it brings faith and supernatural life. But if he does not listen, God speaks in vain and a darksome tragedy begins to unfold. Throughout the Bible we find man faced with this crucial choice.[8]

Of all human activities, man's listening to God is the

supreme act of his reason and will, charged with conscious homage to the God who speaks. But it presupposes the gradual inner growth, under the influence of grace, of an innate and uncorrupted inclination toward God.[8]

I believe that the problem of religion today is to be studied and solved mainly on the level of man's religious sense. For if this is lacking, what value do our religious practices have? We are then fit only for our Lord's admonition, "This people honors me with their lips, but their heart is far from me." [8]

Furthermore, in times such as ours, if the religious sense fails, religious practice also ceases.[8]

This, in my opinion, is now a point of capital importance.[8]

Our main problem today is, therefore, to re-educate the modern mind to think in terms of God.[8]

Considered merely as an instinct, the religious sense is quite primitive. It must be integrated with the development of the higher faculties of the intellect and will, and for the purpose of action it must be directed by the mind. This sense is not only a natural and spontaneous element in the human psyche but a perfectly logical one, legitimate and necessary as well. It has been equated far too often with the human spirit's more elemental expressions on a primitive, infantile, naïve and superstitious level. It needs to be accorded its proper place and function.[8]

Spontaneous expression is not enough. Left to itself and its own impulses the religious sense can lead to aberration, to whim, and superstition, to a deplorable and dangerous pietism.[8]

Moreover, the religious sense is not restricted by the measured, logical pace of the critical intelligence. It soars up into the world of poetry and prayer and attempts to reach an end above anything that is clearly and immediately apprehended. To attain this it needs guidance.[8]

A correct and sure evaluation both of man and of human life is desired by mature critics of modern thought, as well as by personal experience stimulated by social development. Man today needs to recover this evaluation. He needs enlightenment that he cannot find by himself.[10]

People who are insensitive to religion are not creatures who have been liberated from some atavistic inferiority complex. They are rather diminished and atrophied human beings.[8]

This greater freedom they seem to enjoy is the freedom of the ignorant man who does not know the rules of the game and yet considers himself an expert.[8]

Fear of any kind, especially of religion, once it becomes a decisive factor in a man's life is, like all reflex emotions, a fruitful source of disturbing political expressions. Out of these, secularism makes a destructive amalgam, which does not unite the vital forces working for the common good but rather detaches them from their spiritual context and reopens ancient breaches.[8]

But I beg those who have no religion or who are hostile to religion to judge for themselves if they are laboring under the weight of irrational dogmas, of contradicting doubts that leave no peace, of absurdities without escape, of curses uttered in a sense of despair and nothingness. Perhaps some of them have inexact or repugnant concepts of religion. Perhaps their idea of faith is erroneous: that it offends against intelligence, shackles progress, humiliates man, and brings sadness to his life.[10]

Perhaps some are more eager, and therefore, without

knowing it, more prepared to catch the gleam of the light. If they do not rest in idleness and ignorance, the gloom of their atheism will dilate the pupils of their eyes that they may read in the dark the answer to their quest for the source of things.[10]

Atheism, which denies the religious sense, appears especially in antisocial mass movements as a form of spiritual revulsion. People can become so exasperated by an awareness of injustice or by unsatisfied longings, that they turn any doctrine—dialectical materialism, for example—into a fanatical, messianic crusade. From this they draw strength for stubborn, violent, though sometimes impressive action, equaled only by the impact of the inevitable reaction (both on the theoretical and practical planes) against the principle that they have taken as their starting point.[8]

And so God who brings light to human minds and happiness to human living, but is no longer sought for, no longer accepted as man's ultimate aim and object, can reappear in both these tendencies as a source of fear and of profound anguish.[8]

The whole history of religion is proof of the soul's unceasing aspiration, humbly, sublimely, bizarrely, or ignominiously expressed though it be, toward its God. But it would have been forever in vain had not God in His wisdom and goodness taken the initiative and revealed Himself. Thus He instituted one true religion.[8]

Every religion has in itself sparks of light that must be neither despised nor extinguished, even though they are insufficient to give man the charity he needs, or to achieve the miracle of the light of Christianity, which makes truth one with life.[10]

Even natural religion raises us to the transcendent level of that Being without whom there is no sufficient reason for existing, for thinking, for working, nor any basis for hope that is free from deception.[10]

Every genuine religious truth is the dawn of faith, and we are waiting for it in the best dawn, in the full splendor of Christian wisdom.[10]

Spiritual or religious manifestations which do not have truth as their guide offer no guarantee of salvation and are the source of much error, illusion and disaster.[8]

Most positive-minded people today are not prepared to accept spiritual mystification as their goal. Thus they grow suspicious of the trustworthiness of the religious sense as a guide; they grow impatient with its surprising demands and flagrant extravagances. They reject it. They completely ignore it. This explains much of the irreligiousness of our day.[8]

Man's natural religious sense is not a criterion of truth, it is a need for truth.[8]

To stifle this need is to thwart human nature and to do violence to the work and the design of God.[8]

Modern man's main activity is work. He takes pride and satisfaction in it. But it has also made him feel that here alone is power, and this illusion has limited his field of vision. Thus a state of mind is created that easily grows indifferent to religion and, with a little encouragement, becomes frankly hostile to it.[8]

This attitude is not wholeness of mind; it is stunted and one-sided. The human mind can attain wholeness only if, retaining its curiosity and knowledge concerning the scientific laws which are so necessary to man's work, it studies them more closely and discovers that they postulate a transcendent Mind, creating and ordering all things.[8]

Modern man, therefore, must not allow material things, which so absorb him, to blind him to what lies beyond them. A more intelligent response must be stimulated; he must rediscover a metaphysical curiosity, a determination to discover the *raison d'être* of all that lies before his eyes.[8]

The intense research into the newly revealed properties of matter, the urge to produce not only mass "goods," but also works that are perfect of their kind, and machines and products that excite discriminating admiration; the parallel attempt to give to factories, to the tools of work and to the finished article a beauty of design; the desire to raise devotion to work to the status of an ideal—all these are signs of a spiritually imbued humanism which is about to arise out of the materialism of our age.[8]

The implications are tremendous. In this way the material world, far from being repudiated, is ennobled. Human work is not degraded, it is redeemed. And the development of civilization is not arrested, it is baptized and made more truly human.[8]

This speculative movement of the mind which is its crowning glory arises naturally from an observation of what God has created. Could it not today arise from the contemplation of what man has, so to speak, created—the products of his ingenuity, his industry, his tools, his machines? Modern man sees in these artifacts the reflection of himself and is proud and content to contemplate these tokens of his own intelligence and industry.[8]

Is it not possible for the soaring intelligence of man to

see in them a revelation of the mind and work of God? [8]

This is the height to which man must attain today in order to fulfill his powers of understanding and to revive his sense of religion.[8]

As always in the field of religion, this challenge will call for an act of humility—which means, simply, honesty and truth. The technician standing beside his machine may well say, "This is new, this is mine," but he should add, "It is rather my discovery than my invention. I have merely discovered laws and properties that existed before I conceived of them. I have only applied them. I have moved a rung closer to the natural unfolding of a Wisdom which I did not know or dream of. Without expecting to, I have stumbled into the presence of God." [8]

If, in the past, nature was the intermediary between God and the human mind, why may not the works of technology and art serve this purpose today? [8]

This, in my opinion, is one of the keys to the problem of bringing back the lost religious sense into the world of industry and of technology, of science and of art. This is the way to restore a spiritual significance to man's work.[8]

III

THE MORAL CRISIS

Our time, I have always said, is decisive. It calls out for intensity of effort. It invests us with a vocation of preservation and of renewal. It demands the fidelity and the sacrifice that the decisive moments of history have always called for.[11]

But our time is also deeply imbued with the desire for happiness attainable through the possession and use of temporal goods. This seeking for pleasure as the fruit of the conquest of riches, or as compensation for not having yet attained them, has a characteristic and fatal effect on the moral life. Such a philosophy has its own literature, a vast and varied press, almost, one might say, its own organization.[9]

Our time is saturated with the mentality that gives to the sphere of the senses, of sensuality, of pleasure and of vice, such expansion and such importance. Such is the world.[9]

The significance of the expression "the world," as used by Christ and by Saint John in his first epistle, is neither the complex of entities that we call the universe, nor the men of this world, nor even a particular aspect of the human condition. The term refers rather to the mentality and the way of life of those who do not follow Christ.[9]

"The world" is a conception of life lived outside the light of God.[9]

It is the result of ideas that are merely approximative, and of comfortable opinions that are not strained through the sieve of truth. It is the sweep of attitudes unjustly born of comfort and not of duty. It is the exterior and pharisaical form of virtue. It is so-called "loose" morals, which are set free from the strict law of morality only to fall into an even more exigent and overwhelming one, that of the world.[9]

Some of the purely descriptive signs of the moral crisis of our time are the following. First, the refusal to accept what is proposed by authority. Second, the antipathy toward obedience and the law, and a sympathy for the voluntaristic systems of thought, for statism and for totalitarianism. Third, the refusal to accept whatever comes to us by way of tradition, of custom, of habit, with the consequent reaction against conformism, stability and law.[9]

And then, of course, there is the necessity of adapting to the mode and manner and style of what is current, of embracing what one sees will have popularity, of preferring what gives one the return he wants. There is, too, the refusal to accept what comes easily, a rejection of solutions easily arrived at, of what is providential, balanced, of what is consoling to man. And it is the difficult, the problematic, the agonizing, the tormented, the rebellious, the absurd, which is embraced. Lastly there is skepticism concerning the good: virtue, chastity, religion, and sacrifice.[9]

In the world's thinking, truth is not understood as a relationship between thought and reality or indeed a rapport between what is and what ought to be. Instead, "sincerity" or "authenticity" is substituted (Nietzsche).[9]

Truth is understood as psychological awareness of one's own state of mind, of one's own spiritual phenomenology, with the tendency therefore to believe oneself honest and wise when one explores and expresses this "awareness," which does not dictate duties but describes them, and which therefore flees from all moral obligation and responsibility toward others.[9]

At the root of every false concept concerning the human way of acting, there is an erroneous concept concerning our relationship to God. Religion is the foundation of the integral human system that regulates our way of acting. And why? Because God is the first cause of being, God is the supreme ground of thought, God is the fundamental law of human action.[9]

Thus, when God is denied, the whole moral system is overthrown and compromised, morality begins to lack its point of reference to an absolute principle, to a transcendent term, to a necessary obligation. The concept of the good becomes relative and therefore insufficient to satisfy human aspirations. Liberty can become license, and no longer a rational faculty choosing the good. It can become uncertainty, without a criterion for resolving its own dilemma. It can become blind impulsiveness, which loses the dignity and the joy of willing and loving. Thus duty abandons its greatness and its strength.[9]

Even in the midst of so much deformation and contradiction of what is called "the good," there is much in our time that can be praised. There are, above all, some ideals that merit our praise and our endorsement. They are no less human than Christian, derived as they are in their absolute and obligatory formulation from Christianity itself.[9]

These are the light-giving ideas, the strength-giving ideas of modern life: respect for the human person as the source of civil law; the cult of liberty as the source of development of every feasible and honest human activity and as the unsurpassable criterion of responsible morality; the duty of promoting continuous progress in the conditions and in the forms of human living; the ideal of social and international peace.[9]

Justly understood and loyally applied, this latter ideal can change so many provisory criteria and so many pseudo-principles of sociology and of politics. These have up to now often been professed in open contradiction to the celebration, so often hypocritical and rhetorical we must admit, of the sacred and of the Christian name of peace.[9]

And finally, there is the idea of a world in a harmony respectful of the parts that compose it, which does not seem today utopian and oppressive but rather ecumenical.[9]

These are stunning ideas, to which a few more can be added as characteristic of our time.[9]

The first of these is the idea of justice. This idea is an irrefutable argument for the existence of the moral law, prior to and productive of positive law. It is in a state of ferment within our society today, and it nourishes the continuous legislative process which tends to adjust within the social reality needs that the moral sense says are legitimate and demanded.[9]

Another is the idea of truth. The young know of which truth I speak. It is not so much that which is speculative as that which is lived. The ancients distinguished it from the "truth of doctrine" and called it the "truth of life." It is truth stripped of rhetoric, of commonplaces, of conventional enthusiasm and of ambitious pretensions.[9]

It is an attitude of the spirit rather than a logical system of thought. It is born of a disenchantment that the modern world, engulfed in two horrible wars, has inflicted on the generations of this century.[9]

There is an intolerance, a disdain, if you wish, on the part of those who refuse to learn from this distinction of the ancients. There is also the danger of skepticism and cynicism, which can collapse into anarchy, as literature and art at times witness today. But there are also in young and generous hearts a need and a loyal commitment, which salvage the fundamental certainties of thought and impel them to conform their conduct along those lines.[9]

This flourishes especially where the Christian religion is not merely tinseled with exterior honesty, but is a ferment of interior sincerity and truth.[9]

A positive phenomenon that rises from the moral sense of our time and that nourishes it is the instinct, the duty, of offering spontaneous assistance to those who need it. It too witnesses to a humanism fundamentally Christian, and we cannot fail to rejoice in moral and social evolution and not recognize in it a consoling expression of that moral sense that generates an authentic human civilization.[9]

Another phenomenon, which is vastly important in our day and which generates a powerful, reforming dynamism on our ways is democracy. It has been discussed and elaborated as a system that recognizes in people the original subject of sovereignty, and that re-enters into the Christian concept of authority as coming from God. This maintains that when people form a society they possess authority through the natural law, which has God for its author.[9]

But today, democracy has been celebrated rather as a system of organized social life founded on the original concept of the dignity of every single human person, and thus on the process of the gradual emancipation of man wherever he has been deprived of his fundamental civil rights, and of close and responsible participation in the advancement of the public good.[9]

Democracy as supported by the Church is not so much linked to a specific political regime as to the structures on which the relations between the people and the authorities depend in their quest for the prosperity of all.[12]

Democracy can be found in any regime that is not totalitarian. It requires a society of free men, equal in dignity and fundamental rights; a society that takes note of personalities, of responsibilities, and of rights.[12]

Man therefore figures in democracy as a free and equal person, a subject of right, and of duty, in their most complete expression. And thus democracy also represents a human factor of the first order, producing in education and in the spirit of people a moral sense of the highest value. May it, in fact, always do so.[9]

Democracy must be sustained by a vigorous and rigorous moral sense. It ought to be a law not so much imposed as lived; a result of the collective conscience concerning the respect that every citizen owes to himself and to others, and concerning the collaboration and the solidarity of all for the common good.[9]

This interior exaltation of the concept of law and of duty sustains itself magnificently, and I would say exclusively, if conscience is pervaded with a religious sense.[9]

For this reason I believe that religion, clearly understood and practiced, has in our democratic time a new providential and indispensable function to fulfill. I hope that this may be so in order that under the protection of the word democracy there may not be born any hidden hostile elements that contribute to the disintegration of the social order.[9]

Democracy can lend itself to an interpretation which contradicts it. This is class self-consciousness, founded on a concept of exclusivity, and thus of egoism and of collective privilege, and then of social struggle. Or, indeed, it can give place to an equivocal interpretation of irresponsibility and of license accorded to indiscriminate activities, harmful to the legitimate tranquillity of others and of the public good. Or, too, it can express itself in the intemperate interference of a political party which, with the intention of assisting the citizen in the exercise of his civil rights, substitutes itself for him and maneuvers him for ends and interests that are not his own.[9]

When the idea of popular sovereignty proper to democracy does not have in itself ethical and superior juridical principles, it can degenerate into arbitrariness and violence, or indeed into a despotism of a class or of a state. But if it is permeated by a moral conscience, it can favor that fraternity, in justice and in charity, which is the highest expression of humanity, and that has its most fruitful and inviolable source, for Christians, in the fatherhood of God given to us by Christ.[9]

IV

THE MORAL LAW

ALL LIFE IS LIVED under the eye of God. His presence clarifies every particular, makes every act a responsible one. The relationship between man and God is not marked by uncertainty and by fear but by love, the supreme command, the deepest source of our energy.[9]

We know that this relationship between man and God is translated into one between man and man. The love of our neighbor follows on and mirrors that of God.[9]

For this reason the moral life of a Christian will be supremely the most human and most effective in producing a true sense of community.[9]

The moral life of man therefore expresses a dialogue in which God has the initiative: He creates, loves, and calls. Man responds by loving, in a practical imitation of Christ.[9]

This dialogue, the response of man to God, which Christ teaches and assists us in maintaining, assumes dramatic importance because on it depends our future destiny.[9]

The clear and wonderful pattern of the moral life traced for us by Christ is not without a shadow. The shadow is the sin of man.[9]

It is of first importance for us moderns to rediscover the

notion and knowledge of sin. The contemporary world has lost this concept.[9]

Losing the sense of God, of our relationship to Him, we lose also the true sense of sin, which is an affront to God.[9]

We are responsible before God.[9]

In His presence we live our life. Our every act is performed under His gaze. Thus every act should have a rectitude which tends to its final end. If this is lacking, it is specifically privation, it is sin.[9]

This indicates that there is continuously intimated to us a law, to follow and to realize. Conscience is the voice of this law.[9]

Whoever does not follow it, sins. And since conscience is a voice within, whoever does not follow it violates his very being.[9]

Evil grows in us. It is a discord between reason and will. Reason judges something to be good, and the will refuses to will it or to do it.[9]

Sin is an offense done to man, which reverberates in God, because man should respect within himself the work, the law and the image of God.[9]

And since life is all bound up with the external order, with our neighbor and with the norms of human society, the violation of the law of conscience and of the law of God involves usually a violation of the solidarity with our fellow men and of the order in society which we should respect.[9]

Sin thus has a triple malice—subjective, religious and social.[9]

The disorder that is sin touches the world; not the world of being but of "becoming," human becoming, which is what we call action.[13]

It is in this area of our life that disorder is realized, that the drama of sin can become real: our actions can be disordered.[13]

Man's judgment by God will center not on what he knows but on what he does, on how he acts, on that which his will directs, his heart, if you will, his liberty, what we call our way of acting.[13]

It is this that determines our destiny and our relationship to our neighbor, to ourself, and especially to God.[13]

Sin is a disorder which comes between me and God. My actions have infinite implications, which pass beyond the sphere of my immediate experience. If I do something, this has repercussions not only in the area of activity in which I complete it. It is reflected no less on the infinite screen of God. My action indicates a relationship between me and the Lord. There is an order that presides over our life; this is the will of God, which regulates not only what is, but what ought to be, the "becoming" of life.[13]

Sin is an offense against man before it is an offense against God.[13]

The man who sins turns back on himself his own evil action. He degrades himself, he does not consider his responsibilities or even his possibilities. He is a complex of inferiority, which denies man his highest and noblest prerogatives. This denial is a degradation of man; it interrupts his relationship with God.[13]

The God to whom our actions tend is not an impersonal God, an insensible God. He is someone; He is personal. He is that vigilant Presence that is ever watchful over us because of love. He is the God who has given us life and therefore has made us capable of choice, capable of love and of hatred toward Him, and He has done this in order to realize the greatest possible expression of His power and of His goodness: He has created someone similar to Himself.[13]

Man is like to God. The Lord leaves him to act freely, to see if the immense miracle of love renews itself; that is, if man responds affirmatively to the invitation of God, and understands the value of being a man, responsible and free, the master of his own actions.[13]

To respond negatively degrades and humiliates man, offends and alienates God. To live life and to allow sin to come between us and God is to interrupt the current of life that passes between Him and us.[13]

The man who does not have an exact notion of sin cannot have an exact notion of life, of God, and of religion. It is necessary therefore to repeat certain basic notions in the language of the catechism, or of elementary philosophy, and in the language that speaks of our daily experience. Otherwise he may walk as a blind man on the path that leads to eternal life.[13]

We will have no access to redemption, no access to Christ, no share in the benefits of His Cross and of His Resurrection, if we do not have a knowledge of the condition in which we are, of the indispensable need we have of Him.[13]

We are capable of committing sin, but we are not capable of expiating it.[13]

A child is capable of breaking a glass, but he is not capable of putting it back together again. We are capable of destroying the vital relationship that leads us to God, but by ourselves we do not know how to make it whole again. It is necessary that God extend His hand to us, to take us and make reparation Himself—a reparation which we, with all of our penitence, with all of the possible penance we could do, would not be capable of accomplishing.[13]

The need of redemption arises from the consciousness we have of sin.[13]

The atheism which surrounds us and which denies God, denies also that there can be any relationship with Him. But if there is no relationship then there can be no violation of the relationship, which we call sin. Therefore man in abolishing God becomes innocent; he is without responsibility.[13]

It is this lack of the fear of God, the not knowing that we are answerable to Him for our actions, that creates confusion in the world and profoundly changes a people's way of living, of judging and of acting. The Babel that is thus rising before our eyes owes its foundation in part to these radical negations.[13]

A second denial of sin is included in the word: liberation. It is the usual sophism of youth.[13]

Youth, which is explosively exuberant and in which the instinctive is always to the forefront of the intellectual, feels that the moral law is repressive. It feels itself spied upon and then says defiantly: "And what if I did violate this 'no,' this negative standard of life? And what if I should go even far beyond it?" And so it does.[13]

And immediately youth has a sensation of being freed, freed from scruples, freed from fear, the fear of God. Youth believes itself finally able to act just as it chooses.[13]

This form of liberation from the sense of sin locates the person no longer in the logical order, in the spiritual order, the order of will and intellect, but places him in the order of caprice, of instinct, of impulse.[13]

Today a certain school of literature maintains that man in so acting is thus sincere with himself, almost as if by granting to the lower nature of man, to his very animality, rights that take precedence over his spiritual nature, a form of sincerity is expressed.[13]

The man who separates a part of his activity from the equilibrium of the total order in which his life should be integrated produces this infraction and pseudo-justification of sin. And note well that it is a normal way of acting in our day.[13]

Sometimes the words *responsibility, misery, reawakening,* can generate in many a sense of skepticism, of pessimism, and almost of desperation, to which not a few among those of our time are prone. How often do we hear the tedious lament, "But what would you have us do? The world has always been as it is. Nothing can be done. A true knowledge of human nature says that it is composed of weakness and of misery. Why insist on struggle, on fighting in the void, on wishing to be in the forefront of great conquests, when the poor human clay of which we are a part is not capable of standing on its own feet?" [4]

This is one of the facts, one of the phenomena which is most disturbing in the social life of our world today.[13]

How many times we hear it said: "Business is business." And then affairs are settled according to their own law, that is, the law of utility. It makes no difference if in the name of one's own self-interest justice and law and conscience are violated. "Business is business." [13]

A more elegant way of putting it would maintain that the economy of a nation is autonomous, it is king, not subject to moral scruples. We should establish a free economy, and by "free" is meant that economy determined only by the intrinsic laws of profit and of the market place. No one stops to think that the economy, too, is a human fact that should obey human law.[13]

Man is above any economic system. Economy ought to subordinate itself to the service of man, not only subjectively understood, because that would be egotism, but to the service of the entire social world.[13]

A society in which economic legality is not respected is a decadent society, one that is wearing away the sheath of its stability.[4]

Thus, the more one desires economic welfare, and the more widespread it becomes, the more vigorous and spontaneous must be the observance of the two commandments of justice and love. Both private and public education must stress this observance. In the past, careless violations could perhaps find some excuse in the limited economic situation then prevailing, but today they merit an even stronger condemnation.[14]

Political life that prescinds from the moral order does not have laws beyond what it makes for itself. It becomes the art of succeeding, the craft of means, the knowledge of proximate ends.[13]

War and social disorder can follow easily in the wake of such thinking. The wars we have seen released on the world have been caused precisely by a *politique* isolated from basic human principles which should determine the balance and unity of life.[13]

How many times young people say to themselves: "This I must experience. If I have no experience, I do not know life. Evil has its own dynamic, its own experience, its own power. It is necessary to live for a while in its kingdom

even if it causes vertigo." There is a moment of intoxica-
tion, a moment of greatness.[13]

These are illusions! Notice what modern literature, almost by way of documentation, shows us: when it begins
with this principle of tasting everything and wishes to illus-
trate this idea that sin justifies itself, that sin is strength
and a force for living—literature finishes always in a
squalid sense of desperation, and of the absurd.[13]

One of the greatest of contemporary French novelists—
certainly you know to whom I allude—makes a defense of
the absurd; human life, he says, is absurd. Naturally! [13]

Starting with a justification of evil and at the same time
not wishing deliberately to violate the fundamental laws of
life, such thinkers make life seem irrational and absurd.
The strange fact is that these authors seek with delicacy
of touch and with subtle rationalism to find irrationality
in life. Their contradictions would be diverting if they were
not so grave and so tragic.[13]

The awareness of sin gives back to life its due proportion and its greatness. We are made for God. It is necessary to keep this always before our mind. If we destroy in
ourselves the sense of sin we annihilate in ourselves the
awareness of our true end, that is, we destroy our own
dignity, our own greatness and our own destiny.[13]

If we remove the sense of sin from life in order to
simplify it, we drain from it also its dramatic quality, and
the consequences can be enormous and grave. The sense
of sin is the source of moral energy, and if we do not wish
to become insensible, persons to whom nothing matters at
all, egotists, capricious, merely existing, not living, we
should keep it alive and meaningful.[13]

One of the reasons for incredulity or lack of belief is selfishness—not being willing to embarrass ourselves by a word that can change our life. We fear the word of God. We seek not to know it because we do not wish it to disturb us. We seek to silence it because its reception could become for us a commitment, and we do not wish to be disturbed. We have our business, we have our careers, we have our pleasures. "Do not tell us anything that could upset us. We are men of work, we are people who believe ourselves to be solidly placed on this earth." And thus we are losing both the earth and that higher inheritance, heaven, because of our ignorance.[11]

The earth will swallow us and it will be our tomb.[15]

Man maintains a constant attitude of seeking justification for his own lack of responsibility. When he examines his conscience he seeks to absolve himself by his own words of forgiveness. Were he indeed capable of absolving himself, he should at least be able to soothe his conscience by exercising this power. Instead, what happens? What happens to modern man in retaliation for his denial of transcendence and of responsibility toward God? What follows from the attitude of mind of a man who allows himself everything and who believes there is nothing that has any higher meaning to it? [15]

Modern man is in despair, in agony; he is a prophet of the absurd. It is he who derides himself, and it is he who denies his own human nature. He says that it is without purpose, without value, without dignity, without hope, and its end will be a bitter weeping, the ultimate act of all human drama.[15]

The awareness of sin if it comes in the last act comes

dressed in desperation, and, like that of Judas, will be without remedy.[15]

The saints rebel against this pessimistic vision, against conclusions that legitimatize laziness and all its evasions. The saint sees. . . .[14]

He sees that it is possible, that there is something hidden that can be drawn out of this psychology of fallen man, of fragile man, of man resigned to his own weakness. He sees that man is redeemable, that he can be transformed. The saint sees that man properly prepared and directed can be himself a saint, a hero, great, a true and a good man. The saint is a pioneer.[4]

Another disturbing aspect of the world is this: often the world does not know how to forgive, and therefore it condemns. Look for example at the behavior of society toward those who leave prison. The fact of having been punished by society seems to have marked these unfortunates with a badge of dishonor that the years passed in expiation and in isolation have not been sufficient to cancel. The condemnation the world has inflicted on them remains without pardon. Their re-integration in society, if indeed it happens, is done as if society did not know that they had sinned; society chooses to forget. But there is no true forgiveness.[16]

Or then again, the world forgives without condemning. It says in effect: such and such is not forbidden. It must be experienced. Tasting evil has its advantages. One must not become too scrupulous. And thus it allows evil to complete its destruction and to take root even within so-called "good" society.[16]

There is one sentiment that the world uses, but in its

own way: this is remorse. Remorse, which is one of the consequences of sin, is much used in profane life, but it is a use that is principally symbolic. Look at Greek tragedy when it is based on this sentiment. Look at how Shakespeare has etched in immortal strokes the state of soul consequent on evil done. Look also at the most recent and noted novelists. The Russians, for example, in this context have pages which make one shudder, and which are at the same time deeply illuminating. But beyond this the world rarely goes.[16]

Remorse cannot rehabilitate man. It deepens the wound and becomes a part of the one who has wounded himself by sinning.[16]

Thus the world narrows down the notion of evil and seeks to be like the ostrich in the presence of danger: it puts its head under its wing. It does not wish to recognize evil. It seeks to ignore it, it seeks to leave it without words and without definition, and it limits its struggle against it to the hygienic field, to the social field, to some special forms of assistance. But beyond the purely natural field it does not venture.[16]

Another modern form of establishing contact with the misery of the human situation is called existentialism, and it produces a double effect. The first is that of exasperation, of anguish, of distraction, of obsession, of believing that by exaggerating this amplification of the psyche, this psychological sensibility which psychoanalysis induces, one makes the most human comment on the fault committed, and therefore the most effective one.[16]

The other effect is the one youth embraces. It is the attitude that says: "It doesn't make any difference to me." From this there arises amoralism, moral nihilism, which unfortunately is found not only in the pages of literature but becomes a part of everyday practice. Who has not heard of the "Teddy boys" or of the "leather-jacket set"? Who does not know of novels and films and documentaries on this sad involvement of the youth called "the lost generation"? [16]

Today's youth is infected with representations of every kind of crime. The young are diverted to the limits of their capacity with every type of cheap best seller and then we pretend that the child will grow up good, will become a peaceful citizen, honest and desirous of balance in his profession and in his social life.[16]

When we have aroused the young and have filled them with all possible stimuli that find in the depths of the human psyche a readiness to unleash the passions, we have contributed to the creation of delinquents. Then we turn around and do everything possible that there may not be delinquents, and for this purpose we build prisons.[16]

This is the enormity of our actions and of our daily life. We live a kind of habitual crime when we are unjust and when we are sinners.[16]

Hell is not explainable except by admitting an enormity which precedes it.[16]

The natural life we have is a life that is lost. "Who is born of Adam remains Adam," says Saint Augustine; and by Adam he means to say mortal man, man who has been condemned. Saint Paul has an expression that I almost hesitate to use. We are born "children of wrath." Why? Because the full natural order that was elevated to the supernatural order in Adam is fallen, and all of this human becoming transmits a decadence and innate destruction, an essential debility in our very being.[17]

In the Church there is a consciousness of evil, indeed a heightened and acute one. The Church seeks to awaken this awareness, but always in relationship to an order, a responsibility, in a relationship to God.[18]

Such awareness could indeed become a despairing one. Who can make right an offense done to God? Only God Himself! The One offended reveals His goodness. For us, the consciousness of sin coincides with the first act of contrition, with the first steps of hope and of consolation.[18]

Redemption does not change the face of the world. It is not a cure-all that empties hospitals or opens prisons. It has healed the souls of men, it has made them good, it has made them happy, it has replanted hope and confidence, and regenerated those who were dead.[16]

Christian redemption applies a remedy to sin as it is in the sight of God and in the presence of the soul, but not in confrontation with the exterior consequences that flow from it.[16]

We moderns, with so much zeal for exploring our own being, are always an object of mystery to ourselves. We do not truly know who we are. The exhortation, "Know thyself," remains always the great challenge to human pondering.[17]

Who is man? What are we? Do we know how to define ourselves? In the light of the teaching of the Church and of its doctrine, we know how to give ourselves our proper name. We are the sons of God. We are the brothers of Christ. We are members of the Church of the Lord. We are participators "in expectation" of paradise.[17]

V

POVERTY AND SUFFERING
IN THE LIFE OF MAN

THE GOODS OF THIS WORLD can constitute a strong temptation toward the overthrow of the moral order. It is done by way of insinuating a fatal illusion: that the goods of this world are the ultimate and supreme purpose of human activity, that they are its paradise, its happiness. From being a mirror of the Divine they are transformed into allurements; from instruments into chains; from paths leading upward to God to paths leading away from Him.[14]

Therefore the Christian hears and accepts as true and ultimate the word of Christ which makes of poverty the first beatitude of the Kingdom of Heaven. Poverty is a defense which immunizes man against the deceits of this world.[14]

But to praise poverty seems absurd. Riches have assumed such importance that a word spoken in favor of poverty, or even the simple toleration of poverty in our midst, seems ridiculous.[14]

What do we mean by poverty on which is founded the religious spirit of Christianity? [14]

Economic poverty? Yes, this too, but with two qualifications: Our Lord does not impose misery on us; that is, the deprivation of the necessities of life. And second: economic poverty is not presented in the Gospel as a good in itself, but as reflecting, at least sometimes, that other poverty which is indispensable for the Christian, namely poverty of spirit.[14]

The Gospel speaks to us of a condition of soul, of an ascetic poverty, without establishing as necessary a connection between it and the economic condition of the Christian.[14]

It is this poverty, with its roots in the heart of man, that should be preached to all men, whatever their economic and social condition. Evangelical poverty is in fact a warning of the insufficiency of man, and of his need of God.[14]

It is the denial of the primacy of wealth and of the capacity of worldly goods in general to satisfy the heart of man. It is a call to stop seeking fulfillment in this world and salvation from the world's profound and fatal evils, such as sin and death.[14]

It is the wisdom that frees us from our preoccupation with wealth and power, and that teaches us that goodness and love and charity and peace, moral greatness, are not found in money and possessions.[14]

Where there is a scarcity of economic means and a modesty of social conditions, poverty means a dignified and industrious patience. It is a condition for praying well, for working well, for hoping and for giving and for loving. It is a liberation of the spirit of man—which, once free from what is basically inferior, can act and love as a spirit.[14]

We must therefore confront Christian poverty seriously, and never think of it as an anachronism for us moderns, or as an absurdity for those of us who are experts in sociology and economics.[14]

Without this interior virtue of poverty, we cannot attain our salvation.[14]

Wealth owes its value to the service it can render man. But if man does not treat it with a strong and free heart, that is, with a spirit of poverty, it becomes the master and he the servant.[14]

Wealth dominates his thoughts and heart, clouds his vision of life and its direction, dries up the affections of his heart and embitters his relations with his neighbor. It weighs him down with countless cares; extinguishes his desires for the higher things which are his true destiny; lowers his moral stature to the level of the mediocre and venal, or to an egotism rooted in his own possessions. It inflates him with pride and empties him of wise humility. It weakens his will and brings him quickly to a state of idleness, of hardness of heart, of boredom and of vice, and to the forgetfulness of the blessedness of giving without receiving.[14]

And finally, it interferes with the capacity to love—and Christianity is love. It interferes with the capacity to pray —and Christianity is communion with God.[14]

For us, poverty is ugly and repellent. It is separation, privation, weakness, suffering, and abjection. It can be for us an intolerable fate, because it is a renunciation of the magnificent gifts of the earth, a lack of those material, economic and pleasure-giving values that fill our hearts. These values can become our dream, our richness, our power and our pride, and even the indispensable condition of our life, of our progress and of our culture.[19]

But Jesus was born poor.[19]

He who presents Himself as Saviour to the world, as friend of mankind and as the reconciler of earth with heaven, shows at His coming an absolute unconcern for those goods that in general we esteem most highly. He shows almost a scorn, and His total poverty makes us think.[19]

Will it ever be possible, we ask, to reach an understanding with a Messiah so poor by choice? With a prophet so alien to the instinctive aspirations of man? Will we ever be able to listen to, to follow and to love such a teacher? The drama commences here and these various questions will have various replies.[19]

Jesus appears as the herald of a message that remains for many incomprehensible, and one that is difficult for all.[19]

The poverty of Christ is the most intimate expression of interior kinship which He could offer man. Jesus wished to place Himself on the lowest social level in order that no one might think Him inaccessible to them.[19]

Every temporal possession creates, in some manner, division, imbalance and distance between men. Every experience of ownership establishes a "mine" and a "yours" that separates men or unites them in a relationship which, since it is not marked by a true communion of goods, often is not even a communion of spirit.[19]

Jesus, if He did not abolish mankind's right to property, wished totally to renounce this right for Himself in order to come into immediate and universal communion with men, with whom He wished to establish Himself as a brother.[19]

The poverty of Christ appears to us therefore under a

marvelously human aspect. It is the seal of His friendship and of His affinity with humanity.[19]

Poverty was honored by Christ. Therefore we also should honor it. We ought to honor, not curse it, not scorn it as a condition of life if it should be ours, or if we see it in our brothers. We ought to honor it, too, as a virtue, that is as a voluntary disposition that frees the soul from an excessive attachment to temporal goods and that directs it toward spiritual good and toward the practice of charity.[19]

Today poverty is the object of praiseworthy interest. It is studied and it is assisted. But to honor poverty is to do a great deal more than to assist it.[19]

The development of modern civilization under the influence of the Christian message—tacit and denied, perhaps, but real—has reached the point of assisting, fighting and abolishing poverty. But if I am not mistaken, it fears poverty rather than loves it, and judges it as an evil without discovering any good in it. This concern for poverty is indeed a great and laudable thing, a Christian thing. But beyond this point it cannot go.[19]

The complete vision of human life under the light of Christ sees something more than mere need in the poor. It sees a brother mysteriously garbed with the dignity that obliges us to render him reverence, to receive him with haste, and to share with him beyond his due. In the poor, there shines a light; a face is seen which is that of the suffering Jesus—the brother of the poor.[19]

Poverty will be the garment of Christ and of all who are His whenever they wish to imitate, represent, and proclaim Him.[19]

The poor will be first in the kingdom of God, and the society born of Christ will not be founded on pomp, power, or trust in material goods, but rather on the emptiness of this world, on poverty nourished by a wholly spiritual force, with help and sustenance from above. This is the economy of the Gospel, which is perpetuated in the "Church of the Poor." [19]

The Incarnation has been extended to all of humanity and it reappears precisely here where humanity is lacking. Behind the human void, Christ is revealed. The discovery of Him here lends itself to infinite application. He gives our expression of charity an inexhaustible motive of generosity and of sacrifice.[19]

Poverty of spirit is a difficult virtue to practice today because riches—to be attained, conserved, increased and enjoyed—have invaded the human heart.[19]

This is why Christianity languishes.[19]

The materialism of the one who struggles to gain riches he does not have is no different from the materialism of the one who maneuvers to maintain selfishly the riches he already possesses. Perhaps the latter is worse because it is more full of self.[19]

It is Christmas that teaches us a lesson concerning the poor. It is a lesson that begins with a paradox. The Gospel, which honors poverty, commands us to care for the poor, to remove the human evils of poverty, so that in a society that is truly Christian the poor who are reduced to misery, as are so many, should not exist.[19]

Christians: Do not believe that you have ever done enough. Do not ever say no to the voice that begs on behalf of the poor. Have the awareness, the heart, the time and generosity that the great material and temporal necessities surrounding us demand. Do not make of poverty a sad profession of indolent beggary, do not make of charity a source of equivocal gain. Remember the beatitude that St. Paul adds to those of the Gospel, always putting it on the lips of Christ: "It is more blessed to give than to receive." [19]

For the poor, therefore, we should have a special reverence and a great concern. They are the mirror of Christ, as it were a living sacrament of him. They are both a prod to and the object of our charity. They are our brothers, whose needs, even if they give the poor no rights, become obligations for us to fulfill. If we ignore them they make us uneasy, but if we care for them, they are our joy. They are our companions on our journey, always near to us. [14]

Is it necessary to say that wherever there are men who suffer, the Church wishes to be present? Heir to the counsels of mercy of its Divine Founder, how can it remain indifferent when it looks upon this multitude of humans, victims of war or social upheavals, who have been deprived of their country and often of all dignity of life? [20]

Through Christianity, sorrow has become sacred. At one time—and even now for those who forget they are Christians—suffering appeared to be an expression of misfortune, even inferiority, deserving contempt and repugnance, rather than understanding, compassion and love. [21]

It is the patient Christ, the brother of all who are poor and who suffer, who gave to human sorrow its divine character, and who made it an object of respect, of care and of veneration. [21]

Christ not only shows the dignity of sorrow; he calls for a vocation to sorrow.[21]

This call, among the most mysterious and beneficial ever spoken to mankind, Jesus addresses to us that sorrow may rise above the frustration of despair and may become, if united to his own, a positive source of good. It will be a source not only of the noblest virtues, ranging from patience to wisdom, but also of the expiating, redeeming, sanctifying capacity of the Cross itself.[21]

In the light of the Cross, sorrow (and by this we mean misery, poverty, infirmity and even temptation) appears strangely similar to the Passion of Christ, as if called upon to make itself one with it.[21]

The redeeming power of the Passion of the Lord can become universal and present in all our sufferings if—and this is the condition—if it is accepted and borne in union with his suffering. From being passive, "compassion" becomes active. It purifies and sanctifies human sorrow and makes it complementary to that of the Redeemer.[21]

In this context our sufferings become good, and even valuable. A strange and powerful art is open to the Christian; that of knowing how to suffer, that of making one's own sorrow assist in one's own redemption and that of others.[21]

The providential character of suffering leads us to think of the conditions, always so sad and so contrary to the high human ideals of modern civilization, in which many portions of the Catholic Church still find themselves.[21]

The body of Christ is still crucified today, morally but profoundly, in many regions of the world. The Church of Silence is still the suffering Church, the patient Church, and, in certain places, the stifled Church. Jesus could still ask the modern, efficient persecutors of today, "why do you persecute me?" [21]

I am certain that this prolonged suffering is fortified by divine assistance, and comforted by our compassion and that of the universal Christian brotherhood.[21]

I hope that all who suffer in this way may become, by virtue of the Cross of Christ on which they are offered and for which they endure, a source of grace for all who suffer, in any way, for the whole Church and for the whole world.[21]

There is a characteristic comfort that the Christian offers those who suffer. It is the simple revelation that suffering is not in vain. There is a phrase of Saint Augustine that expresses sorrow for those who are ignorant of the wisdom of the Gospel which teaches the sublimation and the redemption of suffering: "You have lost the sense of purpose of suffering. You are thus the most miserable of men." [22]

If men lose the conviction of the worth of struggle, of sorrow, of tears, of anguish, and of human death itself, they suffer a great defeat. Then the pessimism is justified which favors that surge of desperation projected into modern psychology that arises from the question: Of what purpose is life if it is going to finish in such a way? To what purpose is it if it is poisoned by a siege of suffering and of infirmity that cannot be eliminated, and that results in the dissolution of all that we cherish in life? [22]

There are various ways of reacting to pain. One can suffer with rebellion. The man who does not believe and who does not pray suffers in this way even though he is silent. How many times, walking the corridors of hospitals, I have heard and even *seen* this terrifying silence! There are many people who shut up within themselves a sense of desperation, of rebellion, and of doubt without any sustaining comfort.[22]

But there is another way of accepting suffering, the way of the man who believes in Christ and follows him. To suffer with love and for love! Not alone with patience, but with love. This is among the highest of man's activities, which can always be done even when one does not have the strength to say a prayer.[22]

So long as the heart lives it is capable of this super-human act, which sums up our entire spirituality: to love. "O Lord, I cry, I suffer. I lie here inert and unmoving; but I love You and I suffer for love of You." [22]

VI

UNITY AND PEACE

FROM THE Christian vantage point I look out upon the temporal life of humanity, eager to find there a plan of unity.[23]

The vista is extremely interesting, varied and, at first view, contradictory. On the one hand it is clear that the world is unifying itself. Distances are annulled, barriers fall, relationships multiply and become increasingly the material of mutual interdependence. Unity is thus advanced.[23]

But one sees also that this unity is always weak, and perhaps equivocal and dangerous, because it lacks higher formal principles. Such unity can give way to monopolistic or imperialistic or totalitarian regimes even as it can induce a dull and supine uniformity ruled by economic, political and publicity factors. These threaten the dignity of the human person and impede his seeking his true and undeniable supernatural destiny.[23]

Often we see that men are close to one another but not united. A common spiritual principle is lacking by which they can act together harmoniously and with reciprocal advantage in attaining higher ends. Within these, the purposes that are contingent and inferior would find their legitimate dimensions and a less equivocal and fragile balance than we have now.[23]

For me it is clear: the world lacks Christ.[23]

From His Cross a light shines upon the world—it is peace. It is that peace which is the supreme good of human order, that peace which is all the more desirable the more the world evolves in interdependent and communal forms of life. A breach of the peace at any given point in the world today has repercussions throughout the whole structured relationship of nations.[21]

It is that peace which grows daily more necessary and right and proper. It is that peace which human effort, however noble and worthy of praise and support, finds difficult to safeguard in its integrity, and to sustain by means other than those of fear and temporal interests.[21]

It seems almost superfluous to speak of peace today. The word itself is on everyone's lips, and the questions that swirl around it are debated with vast import for the world.[24]

The true sense of peace, according to the celebrated definition of Saint Augustine, is "the tranquillity of order," and therefore the reflection of things that correspond to justice, to the thought of the eternal law of God.[24]

Thus the plurality of meanings with which this sacred name of peace is invested are as many as the concepts of order to which it refers. Peace is not a primary good but a resultant one, which supposes and demands a good anterior to itself, namely, order. And that is what we mean by peace: justice, the harmony of things.[24]

The tranquillity and security of peace are the product of the well-ordered movement of component parts, rather than something which is static and fixed—peace in well-balanced motion.[25]

Peace is not of itself stable and static when the order to which it gives its name is by its nature fluid and changeable. An example is the social order of man. Therefore peace cannot be blissfully enjoyed in this world, but must rather be continually generated, possessed and defended.[24]

From one order of peace another is born. Thus every other order on the human level can follow from the primary establishment of order between God and man, which is the fundamental order. It is because of man's having peace with God that each man can possess peace of heart in the midst of tumult, and that all men can experience peace in their social relationships.[24]

Under the mantle of its humanist and sacred aspect, peace, which encompasses so much, can be treacherously misused by individuals or nations who preach peace in order to weaken those who accept the promise of it, and consequently make them more easily a prey to tyranny and to oppression.[24]

How great a good peace is! It becomes more precious as the value of the interests and destinies it should protect and guard increases.[24]

It is a good that becomes more fragile as the social relationship between the peoples of the world becomes weak and threatened.[24]

Today peace is ominously being founded on the strength of arms—and what formidable arms they are! Peace rests on fear; and if this fear were to diminish, what would happen to the world? And what is peace sustained by fear? A truce if you will, but if it is to be a truce, then it is a vigil of war. And what would be the dimensions of that war today? [24]

True peace is not found in hypocritical propaganda aimed at lulling one's adversary to sleep and in concealing one's own preparation for war. Peace does not consist in pacifist rhetoric; it is not based merely on the precarious balance of opposing economic interests, nor on the dream of proud supremacy.[25]

True peace is based on the abolition, or at least the mitigation, of the causes that endanger security, such as nationalistic or ideological pride, the arms race, a lack of confidence in the methods or in the organizations that have been constituted to make the relations among nations orderly and friendly.[25]

The international organizations, excellent institutions to which I wish an increase of wisdom and efficiency, show themselves incapable today of founding peace on the free consent of the peoples of the world, because they lack a fundamental unity of thought, cohesion of ideas, common philosophical and religious conceptions.[24]

The political positions that nations adopt are able to find remedies and temporary substitutes for peace, and they play the game of international stalemate patiently and admirably, but their hasty recourse to arms foreshadows the tragic possibility of catastrophes without name.[24]

Is it not your mission, gentlemen of the diplomatic corps, to work to destroy the walls that divide nations? Is it not to announce peace to those near and far? Mere words cannot effect this—Christ shows us this by his example, and daily experience confirms it.[26]

The whole person must be involved. It is necessary to be men of peace, completely imbued, if possible, with the thoughts and sentiments that are those of God and that led Christ to become incarnate. It is only in this way that we can effectively announce the peace to others and make it enter men's hearts.[26]

The mystery that is Christmas, it seems to me, throws another light upon the mission of diplomacy. It is a mystery of abasement and of patience, a mystery of humility.[26]

In order to keep peace among men, it is sometimes necessary to sacrifice a portion of one's prestige, or superiority, to yield to a superior good, to cross distances, to engage in and pursue conversations which could appear, in certain respects, humiliating. It is necessary to negotiate, to negotiate without weariness.[26]

And it is necessary to avoid that supreme humiliation that today would be the supreme catastrophe: recourse to arms.[26]

There is no union between souls but through love. If the mystery of Christmas is a mystery of peace and humility, it is above all a mystery of love. To love man entirely and to love all men: this is the great lesson which is given to us by God incarnate; and it is at the same time the condition for the success of the action of diplomats in the service of peace. A diplomacy not animated by respect for and love of men would not be able to create in the world a stable peace.[26]

Is there no other sentiment than fear on which peace can be based? Is it really possible that the whole structure of international order is founded on the volatile calculation of the terror of arms that can bring about the fatal extinction of mankind? And is it not possible to dissolve this reciprocal fear of the probable contenders into reciprocal sympathy and reciprocal love? To substitute love for fear; what a blessing it would be—and what a miracle! [24]

What would happen if the people of the world, instead of hating one another, instead of basing their relationships on force, contending in a kind of egotistical power struggle for the goods of the earth, and involving themselves in strife, would seek to understand one another, to respect one another, to aid one another in mutual need? Is this utopia, or is it not rather the supreme purpose of history and of civilization? [24]

And how can we arrive at this purpose, how can we at least directly address ourselves to it, without a primary and invulnerable principle of fraternity and of solidarity? Without, in other words, the recognition of a common origin for mankind founded in one single divine paternity? [24]

Why are men not at peace with each other? Because their minds are not united. Union of minds is the great need of contemporary man. Culture, which awakens and in great part fills this want, in the end does not satisfy it.[25]

Men lack unity in their principles, in their ideas and in their view of life and of the world. As long as they are divided they will continue to be ignorant of one another, to hate and to fight one another.[25]

The weakness of the Western world is found precisely in its lack of a unifying idea, of a unifying faith.[5]

It is clear that Christianity is still the only sure formula for resolving every human conflict and every human problem. It is clear, too, that it is in the order of ideas, rather than in the force of arms or the decrees of nations, that the solid and simple foundation of peace is to be found.[24]

It remains to be seen how we can attain this integrity of ideas in a world full of errors and of intellectual anarchy. It is a difficult and perhaps impossible thing to do. But it remains a fact that it is in the field of thought, above all of ideas, and of faith, that the best strategy for the establishment and the defence of peace is to be located.[24]

Peace is not only the enjoyment of a beneficent order. It is, above all now, and above all for us Christians, a duty, and in a certain sense the supreme one. It is a duty that is preeminently placed upon those who are responsible for the direction mankind takes, but it is also the duty of each and every one of us.[24]

Peace is not something that just happens. It is created, it is constructed.[27]

Let us pray for peace. Let us pray before it is compromised, before it is broken, in order that it may not be broken.[24]

To pray for peace signifies to open one's heart to the love of all men. We should therefore look with sympathy and with trust on this arduous and complex work, which is also slow and costly, from which a community of nations should ultimately result, not as the fruit of proud and materialistic imperialism but of mutual respect and of peaceful collaboration.[24]

To pray for peace signifies to aspire to the victory of the spirit over capitalistic or communistic materialism, whichever may be the challenge.[24]

In a well-known story of ancient chivalry there is an episode which seems symbolic to me. Two knights are fighting in a battle for the conquest of a damsel, who looks with terror upon the terrible and frightening spectacle. All of a sudden the young woman thinks of flight, leaps on one of the horses belonging to the knights and without saying a word she flees.[28]

She is the image of civilization, which flees when those who are on the point of conquering her enter into combat with one another. It is war that puts civilization to flight.[28]

But what happened in the episode I have just mentioned? When the two knights became aware of having been abandoned by the young lady, they immediately suspended their fighting and, with a high sense of chivalry, they became friends. Both jumped on the one horse remaining and they rode off in pursuit of the young lady who had fled.[28]

What does this say to our age? [28]

The Church considers the United Nations to be the fruit of a civilization to which the Catholic religion gave the vital principles. It considers it an instrument of brotherhood between nations, which the Holy See has always desired and promoted.[29]

The ideologies of those who belong to the United Nations are certainly multiple and diverse, and the Catholic Church regards them with due attention. But the convergence of so many people, of so many races, and of so many states in a single organization intended to avert the evils of war and to favor the good things of peace, is a fact that the Holy See considers as corresponding to its concept of humanity, and it is included within the area of its spiritual mission in the world.[29]

The signing of the treaty banning nuclear experiments

has very intimately touched my heart, because I see in it
a testimony of good will, a pledge of harmony, and a
promise of a more serene future. Always solicitous for
the welfare of humanity, I welcome the echo of satisfaction and hope which rises from every corner of the world.
I express my congratulations on completion of an act so
comforting and so significant, and I pray God that He
may prepare the way for a new and true peace in the
world.[30]

My call is for a united Europe! I cannot but hope that
the process by which Europe must emerge more united,
freer of particular interests and local rivalries and more
tightly bound to mutual assistance programs, may progress
and result in concrete and definite results.[31]

I see, as indeed does the whole world, that Europe is
already a reality to which the development of modern
communication among its peoples gives further support.
The spontaneous evolution of life makes of this continent
a community united by a network of technical and economic relations, which do not ask more than to be revived by one spirit, and to be considered the fruit of a
long, final and enriching effort.[31]

Hence the need to give the actuality of Europe the seal
of the best possible juridical expressions. Those who fear
that the unification of Europe may result in the leveling
and even the elimination of historic and cultural values
of the different countries should, instead of retarding the
process, favor the formation of a sound juridical structure. In this way the formation of a unity established in
the name of exterior and material factors, at the expense
of interior and spiritual patrimonies, will be avoided. And
there will be less danger of its being established by the

force of necessity, to which it would be difficult, to-morrow, to express an effective resistance.[31]

To the reasons for unity that proceed from fact and necessity we should add another: duty. It is the duty that arises from the desire to promote and safeguard peace. The world knows the tragic story of our century; if there is a way to prevent its recurring, it is through the con-struction of a peaceful and organic and united Europe.[31]

Peace founded on the balance of strength, on the dead-lock of antagonisms, or on purely economic interests, can be only a fragile thing. It will lack the energy to solve the most fundamental problems of Europe, which affect all the nations of which it is composed, as also the fraternal and communal spirit that should animate it.[31]

It is not only to achieve this negative goal of survival that Europe seems to be ready for integration, but for other more positive ones emerging in international life, which provide constant hope.[32]

To attain these desirable as well as difficult goals, the psychological preparation must play a contributory, per-haps decisive, role. A climate of opinion, as general as possible, must be created, the tasks to be pursued by the responsible leaders and organizations must be articulated, the knowledge of the excellence of the cause for a unified Europe must be extended to all, and especially to youth.[34]

Thus it is not necessary for me to tell you that I look to Europe with a lively and special interest. I follow, from close by, the difficult, slow, sometimes incoherent course that leads toward the unity, the renovation, the progress, and the peace of this Europe that is so dear to me, and on whose providential and universal mission I, by the light of my faith, reflect so deeply.[33]

I am convinced that the great question of European unity is today a duty to be resolved positively in a measure and in a form which it is not for me to suggest. It must be accomplished by the countries that compose our continent. I believe also that it is the duty of every citizen to give this question the support of his opinion, and, insofar as it is possible, of his work.[34]

Indeed I am persuaded that the solution of the question demands a series of unifying decrees on a variety of levels: economic, technical, military and political.[34]

It demands no less the formation of a unitary mentality, the spread of a common culture. Without this, European unity cannot be truly gained, and when gained for certain determined ends it will be the sum of one foreign element added to another, if they are not indeed hostile to one another: it will be a result, therefore, incomplete and fragile when it is not insincere and dangerous.[34]

One of the defects of modern sociology, a frequent and serious one, is to underestimate tradition and to suppose that a stable and consistent society can live without attention to the foundations on which it rests. To flee a culture inherited from preceding generations is not advantageous to the life or the conscience of a people.[35]

And when this patrimony is rich in the universal and undying values that the Catholic Church instills in the conscience of a people, then to respect tradition signifies to guarantee the moral life of that people. It means giving them an awareness of their existence, and meriting for them the divine assistance that confers on the city of this world something of the splendor and of the eternity of the heavenly city of God.[35]

I am convinced that the Catholic faith can be a coefficient of incomparable value for giving spiritual vitality to that fundamental culture which should constitute the soul of a Europe socially and politically unified.[34]

It is certain that although Catholicism is found only in parts of Europe today, all of Europe draws from the traditional patrimony of the religion of Christ the superiority of its juridical customs, the nobility of the great ideas of its humanism, and the richness of the distinctive and vivifying principles of its civilization.[34]

The day on which Europe repudiates this fundamental ideological patrimony will be the day on which it ceases to be Europe.[34]

Thus the apparently paradoxical statement of Hilaire Belloc that establishes an equation between the Catholic faith and Europe is still true.[34]

And that is why the Church believes that it should and can offer its support to this cause. Its support, as everyone knows, is spiritual, or, we may say, religious, for all those who have the happiness of belonging to the Church. It is offered on the secular plane, too, to all those who recognize the effort of the Church to defend and spread the principles of reason on which nations should base their fundamental humanism.[31]

The Church is conscientious in working for the elimination of misunderstanding and sterile hostility between races and nations, and in contributing toward directing man's steps along the paths of a sincere and wholehearted brotherhood, toward the unity and peace to which Pope John XXIII, with unequaled emphasis, directed us in his famous encyclical *Pacem in Terris*.[26]

Yet, in spite of the hard lesson of modern history, too

many Christians continue to remain deaf to the exhortation of the papacy. How many, for example, continue to shut themselves within the narrow confines of a chauvinistic nationalism, incompatible with the courageous effort to start a world community demanded by recent popes? [12]

But undoubtedly even more numerous are those who have not renounced their strange inertia, despite the frequently repeated appeals of the papacy for "action against every inaction," nor their desertion in the great spiritual combat where the stakes are the structure, the very soul, of the society of tomorrow! [12]

In my desire to extend to all men loving best wishes, my eye seeks to form a view of the whole world as seen from what I might call this watchtower over the world, this lofty position I hold by reason of my responsibility.[25]

The demographic increase of areas where people are starving has not yet been balanced by an increase of the economic means to sustain it, although it has been accompanied by the spread of certain means of information and programs of development, which give to such a state of suffering an uneasy and rebellious consciousness. Hunger can become a subversive force with unpredictable results.[25]

Hunger produces sickness and wretchedness, and these in turn increase hunger. It is not merely prosperity that is wanting to vast numbers of people. It is bare sufficiency.[25]

Anyone who studies this unforgettable and threatening problem is sometimes tempted to have recourse to remedies which must be regarded as worse than the prob-

lem itself, if they consist in attacking the very fertility of
l'fe by means that human and Christian ethics must condemn as illicit.[25]

Instead of the effort to increase the supply of bread
on the table of this hunger-ridden world, as modern productive techniques can do today, there is some thought of
diminishing, by illicit means, the number of those who
sit at the table. This is unworthy of civilization.[25]

Such an attitude of repudiation of life kills the noblest
aspirations of the spirit; while a declining birth rate,
aimed at by such systems, has always proved sooner or
later to be, in the history of the nations, a sign of defeat
and of doom.[36]

Such efforts should rather tend to educate men's consciences regarding the value and responsibility of human
life. They should foster a more equitable distribution of
the world's goods, exploit natural resources in an ever
more rational manner, and protect the family in all that
concerns its inviolable rights and the exercise of its high
function.[36]

I know that the problem of demographic growth, when
unaccompanied by sufficient means of sustenance, is complex and grave. But it cannot be admitted that the solution
to this problem consists in the use of methods contrary to
divine law and to the sacred respect that is due both
to marriage and to newborn life.[25]

I make my own the sufferings of the poor. I hope that
this sympathy may itself become capable of enkindling
that new love that, through a specially directed economy,
will increase the bread needed to feed the world.[25]

I am therefore openly in favor of everything that is
being done today to help those who are deprived of the

goods required for the elementary needs of life.[25]

This is my first Christmas wish as Pope: that charity may reign in the world, that the love brought by Christ, born as a child in this world, and lighted by Him among men, may burn ever more fiercely until it wipes out in our civilization the dishonor of misery weighing upon men like ourselves, who are our brothers.[25]

My universal mission as shepherd of the world makes me look with sympathy and with loving interest on those new nations now attaining that sense of identity, of dignity, and of the ability to function that is the mark of free civil states.[25]

I look especially to the nations of Africa and Asia, and it pleases me to salute their own birth to independence and to the harmony of international life.[25]

It is with special admiration and joy that I greet the reawakening of Africa to civil maturity, and in consequence, to liberty, to independence and to progress. While I recognize the merits of all those who have helped the African people to walk the road of civilization, I nourish the hope that these people may be able to enjoy the rights proper to modern civil society and, assisted in brotherhood by countries economically and culturally more developed, may attain in liberty and peace that prosperity that corresponds to their common human dignity.[37]

I wish to recall with them the source of their vocation to liberty and to the human acceptance of the Christian message. I pray that they may always know where to discover the wellsprings of true humanism, the inexhaustible reserves of moral energy. For only in this way can a people acquire a true concept of human life, and find the wisdom and strength to express in its laws and customs both the great principles of civilization, and the special forms of its native genius.[25]

I know that these new nations are justly proud of their sovereign liberty and that they can no longer permit domination by another state. But I know also that they have not reached that degree of self-sufficiency necessary to enjoy all the cultural and economic benefits of a complete modern state.[25]

It is clear that our own charity, in seeking to discover the great needs of the world, recognizes the necessity of helping these emerging nations not with humiliating and self-seeking aid, but with scientific and technical assistance, together with the friendly solidarity of other nations—brotherhood replacing paternalism.[25]

This is what I desire for these new nations—that they may come as brothers into the family of nations, bringing with them their own civilization as well as their recent cultural and social progress, in a spirit of fraternity, harmony and peace.[25]

The order of love for others, a test of one's love for God, demands of all men a more equable solution for countries in which the living standard is often not worthy of human dignity. All such situations require a voluntary study on a universal scale for the improvement of the conditions of life.[3]

The new epoch that the conquests of space have opened to mankind will be singularly blessed by the Lord if men know truly how to recognize each other as brothers rather than competitors, and build a world order in holy fear of God, in respect for His laws, in the sweet light of charity and mutual collaboration.[3]

My work, with the aid of God, will be to make every

effort for the conservation of the blessing of peace among peoples—a peace that is not only an absence of warlike rivalries and armed factions, but a reflection of the order wished by the Lord, creator and redeemer. It is a constructive and strong will for understanding and brotherhood, a clear-cut expression of good will, a never-ceasing desire for active concord, inspired by the true well-being of mankind in unaffected love.[3]

The Holy See has no intention of intervening in the affairs or in the interests of temporal powers. Its concern is to foster, above all, the profession of certain fundamental principles of civilization and of humanity, which the Catholic religion has conscientiously conserved through the centuries, while it exerts every effort to have them take root in the souls of men and in their institutions.[38]

The harmony of law and of international obligation rests on these principles and their observance, in order that the human family will find that true peace, the incomparable treasure, which belongs to individuals and to nations, and which is so often under attack.[38]

In the period following the French Revolution there were some vital ideas abroad which, by coincidence, were numbered among the great principles of the Revolution. The leaders of the Revolution had, in reality, done nothing more than appropriate some basic Christian concepts: fraternity, liberty, equality, progress, and the desire to raise the lower classes.[4]

All of this was Christian, but in this period it had assumed the dimensions of an irreligious and anti-Christian teaching, tending to denature that section of the Gospel patrimony tending to value human life in a sense that was higher and more noble.[4]

We should take notice of the fact that a large part of our social psychology today is derived from the French Revolution. Developed under the cultural, social, and political movements that followed it, it is impregnated with rancor, bitterness, and hatred. Hence in the progress we make in living together as a society, we are still today poisoned by its deadly atmosphere. We even find ourselves a priori critics and adversaries of civil authority itself, from which we indisputably derive benefits. This is a negative mentality belonging to the past and bereft of many of the historical reasons that gave it birth.[14]

Modern economics and social conditions certainly converge to make it possible for us to overcome such a sad and morbid psychology. They suggest, too, that we give our time a better, more serene, more positive, and, if you wish, a more democratic aspect. This amelioration would naturally derive from human relations, which because of the progressive well-being that characterizes our society are today more equal and fraternal.[14]

It is clear that the Christian social conscience, strengthened by the combination of justice with charity, aims at this, and it arouses in our hearts sentiments of respect for a society better oriented toward the common well-being of all. It can make us not merely cautious Christians, but citizens who are grateful and who are friends to all.[14]

The true notion of humanity is rooted in the concept that all men, different and separated though they be, can and should be thought of as forming part of a solid and coherent whole. All have the same origin and are directed toward the same destiny. All are endowed with the same dignity and defended by the same right, which makes of life a sacred thing.[39]

When the consideration of this human universality forms the foundation of the values and relationships of man, one can then speak sincerely and effectively about equality, brotherhood, solidarity, the rights of man, and if you wish, of democracy, the United Nations, of internationalism and of world peace.[39]

Then there will be no fear of mouthing empty phrases or of confusing these concepts with those of imperialism or communism, which are degenerate forms of universality. And there will be no danger of a dread uniformity, a reduction of every human expression to a single one alone.[39]

I feel it my duty here to renew, to all heads of state and to all those who bear the responsibility of nations, my urgent appeal for universal peace. May all governments hear the cry of my heart. May they continue generously their efforts to ensure for mankind the peace for which it longs so ardently.[40]

May they receive from the Almighty and from the depths of the human conscience a clearer understanding, greater eagerness, a new spirit of harmony and generosity, so as to spare the world, at whatever price, the anxiety and the sufferings of another world war, the consequences of which would be beyond measure.[40]

May they work together more effectively to obtain peace and truth in justice, in freedom, and in brotherly love. That is the prayer that I have not ceased to offer. To all sincere efforts that in our view have this aim, I give my support and blessing with all my heart.[40]

VII

HUMAN ACTION

We are witnesses today to a phenomenon as important as it is serious: the moral sense of the whole contemporary world is in a state of crisis. It is changing. It is neither so vigilant nor so uniform nor so operative as it once was.[9]

In saying this I do not wish to assume the role of seeing good only in the past, and evil in the present, of being a modern day *laudator temporis acti*. But it does appear that a characteristic of our time is the change in customs.[9]

Custom is the practice of a people that, with the generality of its individuals, acts in uniform ways, and that, in its duration, is persistent. It is, in short, the common and traditional way of acting of a people.[9]

This uniformity and this perseverance have a relation to the moral norm.[9]

The relationship should be noted. It presumes that custom derives from the moral code, and that custom serves to recall and impose the moral code. Thus if custom is changing, it must be asked if the moral code is changing, and what expression the moral sense of man is assuming.[9]

Today "action" has acquired an esteem, an importance, an intensity, a possibility of expansion that once it did not have. Activity today dominates the framework of modern life, and everything moves, agitates and transforms it.[9]

Action is today the great criterion of life.[9]

The man who works, lives. Static ideals once dominated life—wisdom, order, law. Dynamic ideals are now the order of the day: progress, renovation, revolution, evolution.[9]

Today, speed is king. Energy, movement, productivity, transformation, domination, provide the continuing exhilaration of novelty and give dimension to modernity.[9]

These are terms that present life not so much in its "being" as in its "becoming," ever speeded up, more and more leaving its mark on what was once considered unchanging and stable.[9]

Our religion is supremely interested in the way in which men act. Where our salvation is concerned, what one "does" is more important than what one "has." "Action," more than "being," defines whether a man is good or not.[9]

Goodness of life is worth more than the gifts of life and in certain cases than life itself, because goodness is the final purpose of that life and the scope of its being. The meaning and the worth of life are found in its moral aspects.[9]

The Gospel constantly invokes this perspective, which it holds to be a purifying, creative and transforming activity. By it man passes from a state of decline or of imperfection or of inertia to yet another state. He does this through his activity, distinguished by growth and vitality, in which love, as the great lever of human advancement, has the primary function.[9]

In order to discuss the moral sense adequately, it is necessary to clarify certain notions. When we say "moral" we mean by that "human." Today there is a widespread distrust of anyone who makes anything of the moral, almost as if it were an annoying pedantry, an antiquated and artificial way of considering human activity. Much preferred to it is the way of considering human activity under other and more "worthwhile" aspects: psychological, economic, political and scientific. But under its moral aspect? No.[9]

No attention is paid to the fact that it is the moral consideration that reveals the specifically human element of action, that is, the use it makes of liberty, which in its turn calls upon the highest faculties of man's spirit: his reason and will. Thus an act is truly human if it proceeds from a free and personal determination to act.[9]

Therefore, the moral consideration of the way men act should be neither omitted nor discredited. It is the highest and noblest, the most personal and, indeed, the most indispensable means of evaluating human activity.[9]

Work, which is the principal fact of human life, and around which gravitate ideologies, sociologies and economics, is nothing other than the development of human activity in a particularized form.[9]

The mobility of modern life has given rise to certain deformities of the moral sense of man.[9]

For one thing it has invaded the supreme height of human activity, which is thought not only to communicate a more operative and challenging zeal to intellectual activity, but also to detach it from its roots, namely its principles. Thought is increasingly more in doubt concerning the validity of its speculative activity, while it continues to develop and strengthen itself in scientific exploration.[9]

Thought suffers self-doubt and conquers the universe! [9]

Having conquered vast areas of the exterior world with the new sciences, thought does not feel secure in its interior concepts, and lacking absolute criteria it cannot impose them on action. Action remains blind.[9]

The attempt to discover an absolute imperative in moral obligation, while denying to knowledge its objective certainty, can be a noble intention, but in fact it remains weak and ineffective in practice, abandoned to the fleeting relativism of thought.[9]

Human activity has enormously increased, but it seems to have lost the fear that once guided it. It has lost the sense of supreme "ends," and substituted immediate "means." It has weakened the vigor of moral obligation and made precarious that respect for law which exteriorly can guide it, and which interiorly can justify, determine and ennoble it.[9]

Thus modern uneasiness is born; the cult of action for itself is created; the revolutionary instinct, the prevailing of strength over right, all are unleashed on the world.[9]

And all of this frenzied human activity, obliged to seek for a criterion and for its own perfection, seeks and finds it in those instruments and in resources which its scientific experience has given it the power to dominate.[9]

Man no longer is master of himself. But he has become more than ever before the master of all that surrounds him.[9]

He has learned to know his world, to draw energy and profit from it, and to use it. Everything in the life of modern man must be practical, comfortable and functional.[9]

Man seeks the perfection of things for his own use. The useful perfection of things is called technology. Technology has become the pearl of great price, the supreme law. It governs man's life because with it he governs the area of his immediate experience. Science itself belongs in large part within this utilitarian perimeter, which is equipped with marvelous instruments and formidable and overwhelming organizations.[9]

It is here that human genius is more vital and luminous than ever. The works born from this impact of the spirit of man upon nature and on its hidden capacities are immense and impressive. They form our present civilization of science and technology, the industrial society, which places such means in men's hands and demands such discipline from them as to radically change our traditional way of life.[9]

Thus society and its customs are changed: the rhythm of life, its interests, the entire scope of man's activity, are centered almost exclusively in what is outside him, with little time left for an interior life. Today man studies, thinks, works and moves as he has never done in the past.[9]

And from this increased capacity for action and progress there is born in him a doubt as to whether the norms of moral conduct are still valid and wise.[9]

With customs changing, is the moral code changing with them? [9]

The fascination for the modern and the new sows in the spirit of man, especially the young, a sense of dizzy exhilaration, of doubt and of audacity to challenge everything.[9]

From this change in customs a danger of the intellectual order is born, that of changing one's ideas even in areas where they should be fixed in truths and realities which do not change.[9]

And with the change of ideas, grave deviations of a moral nature can follow.[9]

The fundamental error is that of believing that the moral law, which springs from human nature considered in its essential terms, can change, that it is not universal and absolute, but relative to the judgment of man and to the circumstances of his life.[9]

This form of moral relativism is most attractive in our day, especially because it exalts human liberty, freeing it from objective and necessary norms, and giving it an absolute autonomy.[9]

No attention is paid to the fact that liberty is the supreme prerogative of the human personality, a sign of the resemblance to the divine that man possesses, the source of his greatness and of his dignity, the inviolable dominion ruled by his conscience, the luminous capacity that makes man the begetter of his own actions.[9]

But this liberty, great as it is, is a relative, not an absolute thing! It is relative to the good, to which man's will is determined by reason. It is not an end in itself, but an instrument capable of choosing the good.[9]

This good is not irrational. It is not even man considered uniquely by himself, but in the complex of relationships in which he lives and moves. And these relationships demand an objective order, a norm to follow, an end outside of man, within whose scope he must integrate himself.[9]

Liberty as an end in itself is liberty gone mad, it is liberty in rebellion.[9]

Thus it can be understood why the partisans of abso-

lute liberty in the end find life to be a torment and the
world an absurdity. And this is why too, when the ban-
ner of "emancipated" liberty is raised, it is saluted by
the absolutist forms of authority, which are despotic and
totalitarian.[9]

Who would dare hold that the social phenomenon aris-
ing from the present modern organization of labor is a
perfect, balanced, and peaceful situation? Do not employers find it strange that one result of their labors is the
dislike they inspire in the very people to whom they have
offered new forms of work? Though they have perfected
the mechanical and administrative structures, the human
structures do not as yet work successfully.[113]

It is a fact that the social and economic system created
by the liberalism of the Manchester school, dominated
still by the concept of the unilateral ownership of the
means of production, and by an economy directed to private profit, is neither peaceful nor just. It still divides men
into classes basically opposed to one another, and marks
the whole of society with the deep and lacerating disputes that afflict it. These disputes have been barely held
in check by the law, or by some temporary truce produced by negotiation in the course of that systematic and
relentless struggle which must eventually lead to the destruction of one class by the other.[113]

Men have not understood what the papal encyclicals
on social questions continually point out: that the cooperation of religion is necessary to solve the problem
of human relations resulting from industrial organization.
Such religious cooperation should never be used as pa-
ternalistic discipline, or a utilitarian corrective to calm
the angry, subversive feelings of the workers towards their

employers. Employers should determine, with the assistance of religion, the fundamental difficulties of a system
which claims that human relations resulting from the industrial phenomenon are purely economic and can therefore be automatically controlled. Religious collaboration
should suggest to industry what other relations should
complete or regenerate the entire system according to the
vision emanating from the light of Christianity: putting
man first and everything else second.[113]

Today there exists a profound estrangement between
religion and the world of work. It can be traced to the
origins of the following crises in modern thought: first,
the protracted effort of modern thought to intensify its own
rationality, excluding recourse to transcendent principles;
second, its determination to laicize itself, and to be free
from any meaningful consideration of God and of the
resultant binding relationship; third, its turning in on itself to the point of finding itself fearfully alone and incapable of absolute judgments, resigned to systematic
doubt, to skepticism and to nihilism.[41]

There is also the two-pronged effort which modern
thought makes to escape from its own interior void.
Human thought becomes the source of all being and reality: this is idealism—the metaphysic of the gratuitous.
Then, in order to escape from this subjectivist and solip-
sistic labyrinth, modern thought seeks to make contact
with exterior reality by way of the senses, and of the
logical-scientific process, which is positivism. This, it
seems, is a satisfactory philosophy for anyone who is content merely with the field of the experimentally observed,
and a utilitarian use of what is observed.[41]

It is precisely in this stupendous and fertile field that

the world of work pauses and feeds, happy to have arrived at this point, and delighted to have found here a clarity and a richness of data happily sufficient for thought which seeks to go no further, almost as if beyond such immediate attainments there existed only the irrational, the fantastic, the mythical, and above all, the useless.[41]

In this context the politico-social and historical events should be mentioned that, beginning with the French Revolution, disturbed and broke the unitary concept of thought and of life which characterized the age preceding it. A political and social break separated, first of all, the wealthy upper classes from the Church and from the witness of a religious faith. And then the working classes followed the path broken for them.[41]

At the root of the conflict between religion and work, many differences and resentments of a political and social nature continue to smolder. These in turn have generated and formalized a tenacious anticlericalism, which has become almost a traditional obligation, a question of prestige, an unsolvable misunderstanding, which, especially in certain regions and in certain sectors, makes it a duty to nurture fierce resentment against priests and against religion.[41]

The way of thinking that exists today on the part of both management and labor is strongly influenced by the dimensions of the field of observation and of activity in which they work.[41]

This field of observation is first of all outside them. Thus the idea of an interior life will be foreign to their immediate experience.[41]

This field of activity is experimental; it is tangible, and it is definable. Thus they have difficulty in conceiving of the invisible, in admitting reality that does not enter into their normal cognitive experience.[41]

This field of activity is measurable. Mathematics dominates it; its quantitative mass binds it continually to the material. To go outside it, to consider ideas that prescind from confrontation with quantitative measurement and corporeal dimensions, is vastly fatiguing to the modern man who works.[41]

This field of his activity is here and now, it can be located in the category of time, which is lived through experience. Therefore he feels no attachment to the past. He lacks a historical perspective, and if indeed he possesses this, it is usually incompletely informed about what has been, and facilely mythic about what will be.[41]

And finally, the work he does can be dominated by him. This is perhaps its most attractive and most impressive aspect. He feels that between him and the field of his activity there is a kind of personal confrontation, a kind of struggle; almost, one might say, a duel.[41]

Work is great but it is not an end in itself. If it remains an end in itself, it becomes a yoke, a slavery, a chastisement.[41]

What is work if not the activity of man who makes himself the master of things and transforms them from being inert, or useless, into pleasurable things with meaning and with purpose? Work is, in its ultimate expression, the victory of human activity over things. And their conquest by man gives them meaning in life; they bring riches, completion and happiness.[41]

The cycle of human activity is therefore enclosed and circumscribed by the terminus of work—that is, its economic result. This is the definable perimeter of life. This is the proof of human virtue. This is the ultimate expression of the power of man.[41]

It is such mastery by way of scientific investigation, sustained by a prodigious and growing technical capacity, that today has enormously increased in scope and in activity. It claims man's attention, his trust, and his pride, and it is difficult to persuade him to escape this circle of impressions, of hopes and of expectations.[41]

He has such trust in his method and in himself that he finds no lack in them, and he does not admit that there can be reasons and principles and superior purposes that surpass them, qualify them and explain them. And since work is nothing other than the exercise of human causality, it depends therefore on the strength and the will of man, on his efficiency, and on his intention. The man who works therefore feels himself to be the master, truly free and powerful; he feels himself at the very heart of the beginnings of nature.[41]

And notwithstanding the fact that his work imposes a severe discipline, and fatiguing effort, he is intoxicated with his creative and formative capability. He thinks of himself as being the first cause of things, superior to all natural causes, while in truth it is only that he has learned to make ingenious use of them.[41]

He considers himself the beginning and end of all, failing to realize that he is limited by that technical and economic world to which he has restricted his vision. He cannot conceive of causes that are superior to him. And if he is challenged to acknowledge another causality that transcends him, he doubts, he rebels, he forgets, and he denies. Purpose, he insists, begins and ends with him.[41]

This I think is the reason why the worker is not religious. He considers himself self-sufficient—he is content with himself. It is here, I believe, that Marxist atheism has its beginning. Marx writes: "From the fact of the self-sufficiency of man, from the fact that man has become sensible and visible in nature, it is practically impossible to ask if a being exists outside nature, a being placed above nature and above man." [41]

Work, it is true, is a secular activity, but it is human too. Human work is guided by a spiritual faculty, intelligence, which stamps the activity of man with the imprint of thought. Thought is the element that confers a human aspect on work; it mirrors it, and gives it its own stamp. Today thought, especially scientific thought, is guided by principles that demand the absolute, that are founded on an inner necessity.[41]

And thus without being aware of it, we are in the area of religion—we are in the presence of God.[41]

With regard to the connection existing between "necessity" and the recourse of thought to God who is the principle of it, Galileo affirmed that in mathematics (and where today does mathematics not enter?) our cognition "equals that of the Divine in objective certainty since it reaches an understanding of necessity and thus becomes a participant in divinity." And Galileo affirmed this simply because the human intellect understands the nature of numbers! [41]

Something similar could be said when work tends to its highest expression, which is perfection. Perfection is a term that expresses hunger for transcendence. It touches mystery because it reflects a mysterious beauty, a metaphysical harmony which, to those who know how to receive it, expresses a divine message.[41]

What does an artisan or an engineer seek when he works and sweats to impart to his product a particular form and function? He is seeking to impress his idea on his material. And what characteristic does the idea, brought to actuality by the material, need to have? Perfection. And what is perfection if not an attribute of the First Being? Does man know that he has before him, almost springing out of his hands, neither a simple mass of material nor an idol—but a mirror? Yes, a mirror— made by him from a ray of divine perfection.[5]

Does he know that while he works he prays? [5]

Each of the two categories of work, management and labor, have in their thinking about religion and the Church, certain specific objections, which are peculiar to their class.[41]

The point should first be made, however, that the workers were not the first to abandon religion. It was the industrialists and economists of the last century who dreamed of founding progress, civilization and peace outside of God and without Christ.[42]

Management offers work the fruit of its thought, its study, its science, its technical application, and of its organizational capacity, both economic and structural. It is still easily paralyzed by rationalist objections, by the illuministic claim to know more with the scientific and practical mind than all of the prophets of religion.[41]

For such a mentality, religion cannot withstand the test and the confrontation with modern rationality. Religion is overcome, religion is explained away, religion is made a useless vanity. Only science matters.[41]

For those who think this way, religion is a surrogate of thought. It is valid enough for primitive times, and for the lower classes, if you will, and therefore useful as a factor in establishing order and morality. It can be decorative and folkloristic; a religion of the people, an ingenuous and sentimental practice, but certainly not rational, not scientific, good only for those who do not know how to be intelligent and progressive.[41]

The working class, for its part, offers a practical and formidable objection which is rooted in its spirit, trained to an uncomplicated and tenacious way of thinking. It is, that religion distracts them from what they should prize above all, from their true economic and social concerns.[41]

Religion, according to this way of thinking, entraps the laboring man. It deludes him, it soothes him; it fixes him in a social, juridical system in which others live in abundance, in security, in pleasure and in privilege, while he lives in drudgery and in subjection.[41]

Religion for him is the accomplice of this blatant, social inequality. It is wedded to a status-quo mentality, dedicated to the sacrifice of the laboring class and to the profit of the capitalist class.[41]

Thus each of the two categories expresses its own objections to religion. The managerial class accuses religion but especially the Church in its doctrines and its modern social teachings, of favoring the poor, of being on the side of the less fortunate, of the working class, and of fomenting by such an attitude demagoguery and class struggle.[41]

The working class accuses religion and, again, especially the Church of favoring the rich, the "in group," and of defending their privileges; of profiting from their friendship, of forgetting the sufferings of the poorer classes, and the precarious and needful condition of an entire social stratum.[41]

The former position, as a further prop to its thinking, accuses the Gospel of not valuing sufficiently the importance of economic factors and the demands of economy. The working class accuses the same Gospel of preaching the blessedness of poverty, of recommending resignation, of preaching nonresistance and of embracing renunciation and pain as worthy forms of life.[41]

I would like to mention certain practical objections of a general nature which are advanced against religion—objections that seem to me to be common to all the various divisions of the world of work, and not only to the two, capital and labor, as the old socialistic theories have conditioned us to conceive of it.[41]

The first is alienation. What does religion have to do with work? The modern world is given more and more to establishing distinctions between the various things, activities, competencies, and qualifications of the elements that compose society. Society is becoming more specialized.[41]

Today these two forms of thinking and acting that are religion and work are estranged from one another. Why confound or confuse the sacred with the profane? Why join the quest for the kingdom of heaven to that for the kingdom of earth? Two diverse finalities or purposes distinguish these two quests. Is it not better if they ignore one another? [41]

The secular conception of modern society penetrates everywhere, and gradually suppresses the religious conception of the world. It is possible to live, it is said, without religion.[41]

The second objection poses the question: What purpose does religion serve? Its uselessness seems obvious to those whose life does not transcend the temporal. Work occupies this sphere, and its standard of judgment is centered in economic and observable utility.[41]

Religion is outside this sphere. Is it not an escape from meaningful experience, a loss of time, a useless involvement? [41]

Would it not be better to be delivered from these sentiments called religion and proceed on the road of our *real* life; that is, the economic, technical, industrial, political, social, etc., without the embarrassment of these indefinable spiritual and religious preoccupations? [105]

A third objection is raised. Religion is incomprehensible in its doctrine, in its rites, even in its organization. This is especially true of the Catholic religion, which is not content to express ideas obscurely, but gives them precision, sometimes even in dogmatic statements. It is not content with sentimental effusions, but demands clear and firm acts of the mind and of the will. It does not limit itself to vaguely uplifting exhortations, but demands a continual observance of determined precepts.[41]

How can religion be a comfort for a man tired from his work when it presents itself in terms that are so complicated and so demanding? [41]

Diversion at the cinema, a sporting event, an excursion into the country—surely these are more restorative to a man who has passed the whole week in bondage to the deafening and monotonous movement of a machine, or seated at a desk engulfed in paper work? Do not these serve man better than the mysterious atmosphere of a church? [41]

These objections, valid or not, exist. They are not resolved by keeping silent about them, or by pretending
they have been resolved. Their solutions will be cautious,
slow and difficult. Whoever wishes to reestablish harmony
between religion and work must exhaust himself in
thought and action, taking care not to exclude from his
consideration a knowledge of the terms involved.[41]

It will mean engaging individuals in a convinced, happy,
coherent testimony of faith in the Gospel of Christ, to
swell the ranks of those that are not insensible to Christian values; a testimony composed of example, of generosity, of reciprocal and fraternal charity, for the purpose
of uniting minds in mutual understanding, and of overcoming the obstacles of egotism and separation.[111]

Even in this sector of life there should be great regard
for two decisive and mysterious factors: the liberty of
man and the action of divine grace. The reconciliation of
the worlds of work and religion cannot come about except
as a spiritual fact. It is for us to create a proper climate
for its normal development. But this cannot be done by
ignoring the inner resistance, the honest difficulties, and
the difference of attitude that will confront it on the part
of alienated man.[41]

Is there something in the doctrine and the life of our
religion, that is, in the Church, that is contrary to work?
To work in its scientific and organizational phase? In its
technical and executive phase? When has the Church ever
been opposed to this normal and proper form of human
activity? [41]

If the Church's end is spiritual and transcendent, this
does not mean that it denies less exalted ends that are
proper to human nature. These, too, would receive their

impetus, direction and sublimation if inserted in a design of life that is larger than that circumscribed by the temporal order.[41]

If opposition does exist, it is because the Church refuses to accept as proper and just a limiting of the human dimension to a material, economic, and temporal horizon. It will not tolerate the taking away from man who works the desire, and also the right, to pass beyond the sphere of his labors and of the elementary satisfaction of the material needs of his life, thereby denying him access to the higher reaches of the spirit of man and the hope of fulness of life beyond the grave.[41]

Why should work be excluded from these limitless horizons, from this intoxicating joy, when indeed it is work that is the most ardent and most assiduous explorer of nature, that is the work of God. Is not labor already launched on its trajectory that leads to religion? Why block its path? [41]

We hear so much talk today that the world of labor is divided. Many battle against us; many march in other organizations. Nevertheless, they share many of your desires, your sacrifices, your aspirations. You must have the boldness of those who possess the whole truth. Do not be afraid you are playing the losing cards. You are love, the future, success, victory. They are automatons. They crush their adversaries; if they won we would all be crushed. But our victory will not damage others.[42]

However, we do not want so much to win as to convince; we wish the others to share our joy, our life, our liberty, our well-being, our future. We wish them to be at peace with us. And we will pray for them and tell them, "Brother, come with us if you have lost your way!" We do not want a selfish class struggle. Christ is with us all.[42]

No misunderstanding should exist between the Church and the working class, between the Church and our time, which demands justice and peace, which marches toward technical progress. The Church has always given proof of the energy and clarity with which it upholds the rights of workers. Surely it cannot be accused of being against social progress as though its exclusive concern were with the higher benefits of religion, with a corresponding indifference for the aspirations of the humble who thirst after greater temporal well-being.[43]

So far as our own field of action is concerned, I should like to see the workers given every assistance, social, professional, and religious. I should like them to realize not only the wrong done to them by forcing on them a materialistic view of life, but that the Christian view of life has far more respect for them as persons and, while allowing for their attainment of every legitimate temporal good, also recognizes in them the treasure of a soul that thinks and prays and believes.[8]

I should like to see technical schools helping them to realize that there can be a vocation, a redemptive value, a religious dignity in human work. I should like their days of rest to be sacred and inviolable. I should like their public holidays to be marked with flowers and song and thought and prayer, and to be truly occasions for recreation of the spirit. I should like to see prayer once again linked with work, sustaining it, ennobling it, sanctifying it.[8]

The working people are on their way toward such a spiritual outlook, and the Church of Christ looks forward to its attainment.[8]

The Church, I say, has understood the heart of the people in past centuries, as also in our day, with an impetus of love which has given birth to so many forms of assistance and of modern education.[41]

It has understood and it has affirmed hundreds of times principles that are unchangeable; discovered errors that study and experience confirm to be such; encouraged movements that express themselves first in the purity and enthusiasm of an idea, and then in the practicality and difficulty of realization. In short, it has opened a dialogue with the working classes, one full of goodness, of consolation and of friendship.[41]

Whatever may be the changing face of the social and political scene, whatever may be the explainable diversity of tendencies and of expressions in the area of Catholic concern, the Church will keep faith with its own word. It will keep faith and will stay at the side of those who work, to comfort their hopes and their pain, to defend their rights and legitimate aspirations, and to guide their footsteps on the path of honesty, of justice and of peace.[41]

The Church certainly will not descend into controversies that are purely temporal. It will not deduce from its principles practical conclusions, which in the economic order can be optional and numerous, and it will therefore leave such liberty of discussion and of resolution to those who have specific competence in the civil and political sphere. But it will seek to illuminate, by the light of its social doctrine, the way that men of good will take, even in the civil and political sphere. This doctrine—and this should be stressed—rests upon the principle of the perfectibility of mankind and therefore on the idea of progress.[41]

When the techniques of productivity have been pushed to the highest point, when the machine has truly been put to the service of man, it will still be necessary to choose between a materialism that would content itself with more refined and easier enjoyments, and a new humanism solicitous for spiritual values.[114]

The light of Catholicism will enter into the world of work particularly through a just application of the social doctrine of the Church.[43]

If we do not wish work to become a prison, it is necessary that beyond the sphere of human activity there open up the vision of the spiritual life. And if we do not wish this vision of the spiritual life to be an empty unreality, studded with illusory dreams, it is necessary that it be illuminated by the supreme and shining reality of the Living God.[41]

The social doctrine of the Church has never denied the function of private initiative in the economic ordering of a nation. Nor has it denied the necessity that the personality of the one who creates and directs an undertaking be allowed to give expression to his originality and capacity. This can be done provided that it is not done at the expense of human dignity, and of the legitimate aspiration of as many as enter into the productive complex of a business, not as servants but as men who are free and who are brothers.[41]

A program of full employment can never reach the point of submitting the fundamental liberty of the spirit to the laws of productivity, under pain of assaulting the dignity of the human person. There is no question then of passing from liberty without law to law without liberty, but of permitting everyone to contribute by his free work to the pursuit of the common good whose demands impose themselves on all workers, whatever the sphere of activity they apply their intelligence to, or expend their energies on.[114]

The opposition which has been created between religion and work derives principally from a too-narrow concept concerning religion. It is conceived as a particular and restricted activity of man, like so many others limited to its specific field, to its concrete forms and its determined moments, and that it is good as a human activity and nothing more.[41]

Yet while saying this it should also be pointed out that an instinctive dynamism animates the economic mentality of modern man, who is no longer so tenaciously attached to his possessions. He acquires them, changes them, disposes of them with great indifference. Abundance has diluted in him the unyielding hardness of avarice, and confidence in prosperity has made it easier for him to spend, to share and to risk. There is a consonance here with the Christian mentality insofar as it tends to consider temporal goods as means, not ends.[14]

In this world of work where so much has been done to extinguish the light of faith and so much success obtained, it will not be easy to relight it. The effort of thought necessary to overcome modern atheism is no small effort, especially if some of the contemporary prophets of literature and of the theater discourage such effort. "The only concrete problem that I know today," says Camus, "is whether or not one can be a saint without God." [41]

It is not a matter of surprise but rather one of sorrow if a squall of skepticism or interior desperation possesses the new generation and brings a discomfort without name into the depths of the souls of so many workers who curse their labor and dream of the false paradise of vulgar pleasures.[41]

Anatole France has written: "Because of having cried out: 'Blessed are those who suffer and woe to those who rejoice,' the Gospel has reigned for two thousand years." [41]

And the cry continues. Listen to it. "Come to me all of you who are weary and heavy burdened and I will refresh you." [41]

VIII
MARRIAGE

I HAVE BEEN SPEAKING about a mentality which is false by reason of its incomplete understanding of human nature and its uninformed negation of the Christian mystery concerning man.[44]

Among other deviations, it has given birth to a purely naturalistic concept of matrimony. What follows, as so often does in the myopic perspective of logical positivism, is a debased secular concept which seeks to implant an idea of matrimony abandoned to caprice and to the passions of those who enter into it. Even as marriage is born of the free will of the contracting parties, it is said, so it can be dissolved at choice.[44]

If egotism rules the kingdom of human love, which is the family, it degrades it, weakens it and dissolves it. The art of love is not so easy as is commonly believed. To teach it, instinct is not enough, passion even less so—and pleasure not at all.[44]

Love can express the two polarities: egoism and sacrifice. The first tends to extinguish life, the second to give it. Marriage has for its pattern the love of Christ, which sacrificed itself for humanity and redeemed it.[44]

When true love is deprived of its sacred character, of

its mysterious spiritual light, of its lofty reasoned purpose
and demanding moral law, all that is left are the dregs of
eroticism.[44]

At first, sexual energy spoke only with its own voice.
Then it gave birth to a type of literature, of songs and of
films that today holds the center stage in the great theater
of modern life. All of these seek to express what is called
sincerity, normal experience, the authentic expression of
our nature; liberty finally freed from every scruple, from
every restraint and from every moral support.[44]

Living and acting thus, separated from the ancient richness of Christian law, man continues to describe by means
of always newer sequences, but fundamentally always
monotonous ones, a compulsive and degrading descent.[44]

Instinct emerges as master, and at the epilogue of every
drama registers the defeat of free man enslaved by a
fatality stronger than himself, which can give him only
tears to shed for virtue that has been lost, and a voice to
shout against the wickedness and absurdity of life.[44]

These are dramas now so habitual that an immense
publicity is mounted that not only presents them for what
is a seemingly insatiable human need for dream-world
fantasies, but suggests and teaches them almost as if to
make of them a new way of thinking and of life for the
new generation.[44]

One of the fundamental causes of the weakness and of
the decay of marriage in our generation is the lack of
spiritual preparation in the founding of the family itself.
It is usually maintained that nature is the teacher in such
a preparation, but nature as teacher can fail in its function if it is not itself instructed, disciplined and enlightened.[44]

For Christians who know that matrimony has been elevated to the dignity of a sacrament, adequate preparation for marriage is indispensable. This becomes more true as education in the home, for so long a school wise in the ways of life, of virtue, and of habit, no longer has the authority nor the capacity to prepare its sons and daughters for this great act of marriage, which determines their state of life and their future as well.[44]

Thought must be given to a modern and specific preparation for matrimony in which its nature, its obligations and its moral and religious values may be taught to the future partners in such a way that they can found their new family with deepened understanding and fulness of spirit. The engagement period takes on great educative importance.[44]

Every important, beautiful, and delicate action that we perform demands a proportionate preparation. The great and, in a certain sense, supreme act which is matrimony, demands that it be perfected by new family, social, and pastoral guidance as well. A field of sensitive and magnificent work is opened up to the zeal of educators and priests.[44]

It is necessary to have a complete concept of the family. Just because the natural instinct leads to it, it is a facile illusion to think that instinct itself is enough to give to the contracting parties an exact idea of human love and of the family that results from it.[44]

Emotional and sexual experience, it is maintained by many, is a necessary and sufficient initiation. Many of the young are deceived by this attitude, which becomes blind prejudice and hypocritical justification of sexual license. Such experience, which has no moral norm nor spiritual sense, cannot give anything other than a degraded suggestion of the deep unity into which this man and woman could enter.[44]

Unhappily, a sequence of negative results overwhelms those who succumb to this thinking. There is a sense of degradation in the beginning, then of profanation, a feeling of vulgarity and bitterness and disgust, weariness, hatred even, and finally pessimism. Such is the issue of the mysterious and fatal disorder of pleasure sought for itself, the so-called, "free love." [44]

The high dignity of human love must be restored. Dignity, however, is more than honesty. It involves not only licitness, but moral greatness and spiritual splendor as well. Those who are preparing for married life should be aware of the easy, dangerous, and almost always fatally progressive degradation of sexual life if it is separated from the Divine design.[44]

They should know, too, that there is a real and ideal beauty in sexual life, if it is reinstated in the order established by God. We should give them a sense of the risk that exists between the two possibilities. They are like one who walks the edge of a precipice, between the danger of a fall into the abyss and the joy of conquering the heights above. Vice and virtue almost touch one another.[44]

It is an idea that must be their guide, a new idea of human love sublimated by Christ.[44]

This preparation for marriage will be assisted if the formation of a family is presented to youth and understood by those who intend to found a family, as a vocation, as a mission, as a great duty, which gives to life its highest scope and fills it with gifts and virtues. Nor can it be said that such a presentation deforms or exaggerates the reality of things.[44]

Matrimony is not a capricious episode, it is not a momentary adventure. It is a conscious and definitive choice of a state of life considered best by the one who chooses it. It is a state of life which the man and woman create for each other: not only to complete each other physically, but to interpret together a providential design which determines their human and their superhuman destiny.[44]

They seek a fulness in their matrimony that realizes "humanity," the natural image of God the creator, in Himself fruitful and loving; and that realizes also the supernatural image for Christians of the union of Christ with His Church.[44]

If matrimony is so considered, the two great voluntary acts of which the human spirit is capable, love and duty, are blended in a single sentiment, in a single intention. Love follows its proper development, which is to give itself, commit itself, in depth and for always—and thus duty receives its thrust, its energy and its unconquerable strength. This is the life of marriage as Christ preserves it and transfigures it.[44]

Whoever degrades matrimony makes an attempt on the very foundation of society and on the source of life.[44]

Marriage is a free act in its origins, but once perfected, that is, ratified and consummated, as the jurists say, it no longer depends on the will of those entering into the contract. It is a public act, a sacred act, a definitive and solemn act, which imposes a binding obligation on those who place it before their children and society, before their conscience, before their God.[44]

Shame on those who debase it, or who dilute its concept. Shame on those who divert the public by spreading wretched stories of vice which fascinate the public, by illustrating the baser ways of life and the scandalous loves of public figures, almost as if they treated only of casual adventure stories to satisfy the avid curiosity of the weak and indefensible.[44]

Shame on those too, who place conditions to their marriage that wound its properties and its essential finality, in order to make of their matrimony only a source of pleasure and to give themselves pretext for a later attack on its validity. Shame also on those who construct castles of lies and of perjury, or who deform the truth with posthumous and fictitious reconstructions of facts, to mislead the judge into a declaration which will free them from the bond which no one can dilute.[44]

We should habitually recognize and honor the perfection of Christian matrimony, and favor the formation of families in which this ideal of natural and supernatural perfection can be realized. It is not true to say that this is impossible today. I would say rather that this is more than ever necessary in our time, and that it is already on the way to realization in those places where Catholic life is being lived fully and generously. It is in the mainstream of the modern development of Christian spirituality, and it is one of the signs of the times that the family appears as a source of grace.[44]

It is a fatal error to locate love outside matrimony. Then it is no longer love but passion, disorder and vice.[44]

It is necessary therefore to study how natural love becomes Christian love. It is not only in the moral realm that the grace of the sacrament is stamped on natural love.

This is in itself a great benefit, because it obliges natural love to develop according to a design of honesty and of beauty which takes away nothing, and which enhances the native value of natural love. Further it sanctifies natural love and above all it purifies it.[44]

To purify love: this is the great thing! Grace, if encouraged, leads to this end. The various components of natural love—instinct, imagination, sensitivity, passion, sensuality, rationality—are ordered and governed by an inherent and higher spirituality which unifies them and raises them to a supernatural expression.[44]

The sacrament of matrimony places in the heart of the husband and wife a seed, which should develop and permeate all of life in such a way that its various aspects are shaped by an attitude of love, by mutual love for each other and for the children. Thus there is reflected in these daily forms of life the love of God.[44]

In order to accomplish this there is demanded a long effort to submit natural love to the demands of Christian love.[44]

It is not enough to have offered a sacred vow to true love. It is necessary to renew it every day. It is necessary in a special way to give it full freshness on those occasions that are most important to a family: the birth of a child, an anniversary, a time of affliction. It is necessary, especially after some years of matrimony, to strive constantly against the temptations of skepticism, a kind of resigned illusion, of weariness, of turning in on one's self, and of egoism.[44]

The family is constructed spiritually every day, and its value is derived from the daily fidelity to the basic obligation of a love which has been blessed by God. And I dare, therefore, to pronounce a marvelous word in this regard: charity thus becomes love! [44]

A Christian family which is closely united, rich in its own spiritual possessions and polarized around itself, will not thereby be closed off in itself, isolated from other families, from civil and from ecclesiastical life. The love that unites it in a domestic community does not isolate it from the social community. Much less does it convert it into a kind of group egoism. It ought to create the first sense of community, but not stop here; it ought to determine it, but not restrain it.[44]

The Christian family is the friend of other families, it is a part of the larger circle of customs and of laws common to all. It nourishes also the sense of identity with its own country, it loves the very soil of its country, its history, its destiny. It serves the needs of its own nation and respects its laws and promotes its prosperity. It is the school where the Catholic sense is born; it is an introduction to humanity. It is an approach to universal love and to a complete vision of the world.[44]

To Christian families, then, I extend a word of comfort and of admonition. Be aware of your dignity and your mission, hold firm to the practice of the specific virtues that enhance domestic life. May you find in the purifying sources of Christian love their strength and peace.[44]

Do not fear to observe those laws of life that involve you in the continuing creative work of God. May you be able to adapt your family way of life to the new demands of modern times, and may you grow in the understanding of the vitalizing role you have to play in society. May you know, too, that in the Church yours is a place of distinction and of beauty.[44]

IX

EDUCATION AND RELIGION

IT IS A CHARACTERISTIC of Catholic education to draw from history not only the cultural reminiscences of the past but also a living tradition. It communicates a spiritual factor of moral formation, a constant design for progress, which is direct and consistent in the march of time. It represents a guarantee of stability and of duration, which gives to a people its dignity, its right to life, and its obligation to act in harmony with other peoples.[35]

We should remember above all else that the best defense of our schools is their excellence. If the schools are sound and good, if they provide direction as well as education, if they give satisfaction to parents and to society, then they are well defended, and to this defense ecclesiastical authority will give its approval and support.[45]

We might be tempted to think that after so much effort and so much construction, our schools have reached a final standard, and that we can say we have done everything in our power, that we have reached a peak of efficiency; consequently, that there is nothing more to be done. The reply to this is that, on the contrary, we must believe in the progressive improvement of our schools; not in a spirit of dissatisfaction with the schools of the past, but because the improvement of our schools is part of the broader transformation in the life of the people.[45]

The culture that is permeating even the least educated classes has stirred up consciences, opened up new horizons, changed customs, and created a new mentality, so that if our schools wish to keep abreast of the times, they must be willing to change.[45]

We must put an end to poorly conducted schools that struggle for existence, their aim not being sound pedagogy but the keeping alive of a religious community, or providing for the maintenance of other institutions of the Catholic world. Our schools in the hands of responsible and experienced religious congregations or ecclesiastical authorities must not be mediocre; they must strive for perfection in every detail. Our schools must know how to really educate, how to form strong souls, how to form the consciences of those for whom the Christian way of life is not a veneer.[45]

Our schools are attended by children whose parents sometimes undo what the school does; we should not ignore this problem. I believe there should be a little more discipline, more insistence on study, more submission on the part of pupils to authority. I take the liberty of suggesting that relations between teacher and pupil be more personal. To be successful, education must be the result of a dialogue of one person with another.[45]

We must do everything possible to provide, especially for our colleges, spiritual directors who are truly learned, truly reasonable, and able to instill dynamic and strong principles in the minds of the students.[45]

A school that stresses only scholarship imparts instruction, but leaves souls dissatisfied and indifferent.[45]

Having said this, I hope that our schools will be transformed, improved, perfected, not in a spirit of rivalry but in a spirit of collaboration with other schools, including public or state schools.[45]

The intrinsic law of all university life is a commitment to study and to thought, which is necessary in order that it may remain faithful to what it is. It has a spiritual and cultural vocation which it proclaims and nurtures in the drama of its own personal problematic concerning the choice and the orientation of its ways of thought. It has a sense of responsibility to knowledge, to which it feels bound by its own function as a superior instrument in the culture of its social commitment.[34]

This, perhaps, may seem to you a conception of university life that is too intellectual. It may appear to ignore the modern tendencies that today characterize it. These are easily accessible to the younger generation, inclined as it is to a certain skepticism concerning the validity of speculative thought, and to a certain preference for the voluntaristic forms of the spirit or for existentialist decadence, today become almost *de rigueur* in certain student circles.[34]

These ways of thought are derived often enough from influences exterior to the university; as much from the political events of the day as from whatever literary or social style is in vogue; for the most part they are not born of the genuine demands of higher education.[34]

Because of the patrimony of truth that his religious faith gives him, the Catholic university student can draw

on a nucleus of philosophical presuppositions. They constitute the foundation of human reasoning and give to his
studies sureness and confidence, a speculative and constructive capacity as well. This nucleus further places at
his disposal resources of concepts and expressions that
not only assist the formulation of a superior humanistic
vocabulary, but also give to scientific vocabulary the possibility of clear and unequivocal definitions.[34]

And this, more a program than a method, integrates
specialized university study within a doctrinal framework,
which in turn establishes a logical rapport with the varied
and immense fields of human knowledge. The aspiration
for unity of knowledge not found in the one-sided, partial, and close vision to which every university student of
a particular discipline is tempted, thus is located at the
very summit of the ultimate laws of men's knowing. Such
laws have the virtue of synthesis because they are close
to the source of truth, no longer merely "known" but
considered the creative and formative force of the universe in which we live.[34]

One of the deplorable lacks in contemporary culture is
the ignorance of religious truths, especially in their authentic formulation, in their sources, in the patrimony of
Catholic thought, in the expressions of the teaching
Church.[34]

This lacuna can be filled by the study of religion, which
is a precious and integrating element of university study.
It is for you to discover it first and then reveal the richness of Catholic thought, beginning with the elementary
observation that dogmatic statements of its fundamental
doctrines, rather than arresting the dynamic and original
development of culture, stimulate and favor it, as is

proper to truths armed with certainty and oriented to life.[34]

You can further show how Catholic culture is, by its very nature, attuned to organic manifestations in all human activity. It is not an abstract speculation, superfluous and egotistical, but a doctrine that demands to be coordinated in the moral life of whoever possesses it. It demands also a social expansion, an overcoming of the instinctive confines of individualism, of economic utility, of timidity, and of the incapacity for expression, that it may be a gift to our brothers and a light to society.[34]

In this context it should be observed that Catholic education offers to Christians a universality full of secure and original content, which the seekers of universality outside of Catholicism are obliged to sacrifice. Their universality becomes generic, often equivocal and reduced. It is content with simple symbols; at other times with humanitarian, irenic, and ingenuous expressions of universality. The pan-Christian and ecumenical movements sometimes create an appearance of catholicity that damages truth and fidelity to the richness of doctrine and to the moral commitment of Christianity that they seek to affirm and to promote.[34]

Today, more than ever, man is tempted to adore himself, and to make of man the supreme end of philosophy and of history. Today the belief is common that man can by himself, using only his own powers, progress and save himself. In other words he seeks his own glory and not the glory of God.[24]

This tremendous and fateful change in the axis of human living is happening before our very eyes. From being

theory, the denial of God is becoming practical. Once restricted to relatively few who were intoxicated with speculative utopias, it is today becoming a myth of the crowd.[24]

A humanistic spirituality is being affirmed, which is
profoundly egoistic because it is shut off from the love of
God, and it is radically revolutionary because it is shut off
from the hope of God.[24]

Man is by his very being meant to transcend himself:
he is a being projected towards God, ordained to God. If
this fundamental destiny of man is denied, the luminous
mystery of God-made man will no longer be celebrated
as a feast of happiness and of peace. And the darksome
mystery of man who makes himself God will be a tragedy
productive of inconceivable disaster.[24]

The duty and the need to give to the religious problem
of today a valid solution are not relevant to the man of
yesterday alone but to men of every time. If the man of
today is less sustained by the solution that past generations have given him, the duty and need increase in him
to give to the religious problem its true response.[46]

And if the reply is a truth not born of current fashion
nor the caprice of human versatility, nor of the restlessness of our disquiet, but is a permanent truth offered by
God himself to our tortured seeking, to know it is not
to be stupid but to be wise. It is wisdom to hear it and to
live it, today as yesterday, today even more than yesterday! [46]

How has God appeared in our world? Two aspects of
His appearance seem to me worthy of our attention. The
first is that He has appeared historically, that is, in a given
moment, in a given place and in a given form. He has

inserted Himself into the drama of human life, indicating
thus the point of contact between religious and philosophical thought, and history, between the religious idea and
the religious fact. Second, He appeared humbly, that is,
without noise, without violence, without exterior trap-
pings, without dominating exteriorly that world and that
history in which He made Himself present.[47]

That is to say that the quest, now made secure, for
fulfilment in God ought to be centered less on pathways
of speculation and of miracle than on that human figure
who is unique and worthy of unending contemplation.[47]

At the end of a purely natural seeking after God His
name is mystery; at the beginning of Gospel history His
name is Jesus.[47]

Christmas is the feast of the arrival of Christ, the Word
of God made man. It is the celebration of the great voyage
that the Son of God has completed to draw near to us.[46]

Christmas celebrates the intention of God to transcend
distance, to leap across the ineffable abyss of His transcendence and to bring Himself so close to human life as
to make it His own. It is His intention to make us His
brothers, to live and dwell with us, to enter into our experience, to humble Himself to the level of our sufferings
and to take upon Himself our sins. Christmas is the
mystery of religious nearness, of divine accessibility, of
brotherhood with Christ and therefore of communion with
God.[46]

This is a beautiful way of expressing it for those of you
who are not accustomed to religious expressions, because
in effect Christmas says: "Are you looking for God? You
will find Him in man!" Yes, He has Himself become man.

This indicates that the face of man, made, as we know, to the image and the likeness of God, is here made equal to that of Christ.[46]

Man becomes my brother and becomes the object of my religious seeking. If I have the intention of remembering that the face of Christ is best revealed where the face of man is suffering and in need, then this is the way in which the religious life is most directly revealed to me. It is the way of charity, of doing good, understood in its widest sense as done for a spiritual and religious purpose; that is, for the love of Christ and God.[46]

What God has done for us in His Incarnation seems almost excessive. It seems too much that Christ has been made for us. Having discovered the fire—because He *is* fire—we fear the fire. A religious contact that is so intimate, and offered in such a way, makes us fearful. An act of courage is necessary to accept a religion which manifests itself as a mystery of divine love extended to the whole of mankind and to each single soul.[47]

The universality of the redemption of Christ is among the greatest truths that have ever been announced to mankind. It is at the very soul of the modern conception that seeks the unity of the world, the equality of peoples and the fraternity of man.[48]

It is the doctrine that makes privilege and arrogance collapse, as well as dictatorships, tyrannies, imperialism, and colonialism. It rouses respect for the human personality in whatever life it takes root. It sustains the supremacy of law over force, promotes liberty and justice among men and is the foundation of a true, positive and progressive democracy, rooted in the rights of people and of their public and private relationships with each other.[48]

If the relationship with God established by the Redemption is forgotten or denied, discrimination, social and national contention and hostilities, war itself, can always advance claims which are superficially unassailable, to justify themselves and to compromise the fundamental basis of human brotherhood.[48]

How many there are who live outside the religious sphere and think themselves free, or excluded, or incapable of crossing the threshold of religion! [47]

They are the thinkers who have constructed for themselves ideological systems, presuming them impregnable against the intrusion of Christian thought. They are the practical men of affairs who believe that they can contain all of reality within the scope of economic calculations foreign to spiritual values. They are the politicians who consider themselves absolutely obliged to defend themselves against the sovereignty of religion, or who believe that they can interpret history and the social order with dogmatic principles that are less definitive.[47]

Do not all of these seekers after truth see that it is precisely certainty that is lacking to them, and that the very absence of Christ from their systems is an invitation to Christ? They believe Him to be far away and He is instead close to them.[47]

God in the very act of revealing Himself remains mysterious. The manifestation of God is never separated from a veil of mystery. Revelation is a shining cloud because the Divine Reality exceeds our capacity for comprehension. "If you think you understand, it is not God Whom you have understood," says Saint Augustine. And, too, the Lord has always wished that the acceptance of His revelation be a free act, a meritorious act, an act by which man makes his own choice and thus participates, in some measure, in the work of his salvation.[49]

This means that the good fortune of accepting His revelation, of believing and of entering thus into the blessed circle of communication with the very life of God, on the one hand is a free and perfect gift of God, and on the other demands the cooperation of our total selves. But this duty of seeking will differ in the believer and unbeliever.[47]

This diversity in seeking gives rise to a specious and dangerous objection which is dear to many modern intellectuals. It maintains that seeking the truth is worth more than the possession of the truth because the possession halts the movement of the spirit, whereas the seeking stimulates it and is exacting.[50]

This is false and even unjust when it is applied to the believer as contrasted with the nonbeliever. It is the same as saying that the believer, surfeited by certainty already attained, and committed to dogmatic teaching, can have no more incentive for intellectual and spiritual activity, whereas the nonbeliever, beginning with uncertainty and the liberty that derives from it, would be more moved to seek the fulness of thought and of interior experience.[50]

The assertion is false also because truth once possessed does not hinder but provokes the conquering drive of the spirit. Truth is productive, not sterile. Thought proceeds from certainty possessed to certainty to be possessed. Logic is founded on this principle. Knowledge feeds on its own development and grows from its own progress.[50]

Religion therefore is its most valid nourishment. From one conquest of divine truth it is possible to attempt to learn a second and a third. It is possible to derive a moral law and a prayer, a greater desire, a greater thirst and a greater love from the primary conquest.[50]

The formulation of religious truths in exact terms, that is, the presentation of a new dogma in our faith, does not dry up thought on that truth and does not suffocate prayer.[50]

Do not make of the blessing of the faith and of the teaching of the Church that you possess a motive for not seeking to progress in the knowledge and in the understanding of the things of God.[50]

The act of faith does not dispense us from a study of religious truths, and thus meditation is born. It does not dispense us from love of religious truths, and thus prayer is breathed. It does not dispense us from conformity to religious truths, and thus virtue and the Christian life are communicated to the world.[50]

For those who do not possess the faith, there is a duty also. Those who are in darkness must seek the light, and this duty is nothing other than a man's regard for his own probity; that is, the honest use of thought.[50]

Thought is by its nature oriented toward the truth, even if it is easy to lose oneself in the act of seeking. The man who overcomes weakness, deviation, utopias, fantasies, hypocrisies, utilitarian calculations, blindness, ironies, sophisms and lies in his search for truth will in all probability find it.[50]

He who respects his own thought is already in the way of truth.[50]

The religion that we have the good fortune to profess, is, in effect, the supreme science of life. It is, therefore, the highest and the most rewarding teacher in all the areas where life manifests itself. It could well appear to be absent when it not only permits but actually commands the intellectual to obey only the laws of truth.[51]

But if he looks closely, he will see it near him, encouraging him in his difficult exploration, assuring him that truth exists, that it is intelligible, that it is magnificent and divine. It will remind him at all times that thought is an instrument proper to the conquest of truth and that it must be utilized with such a respect for its proper laws that one continually feels the acceptance of a responsibility that engages and transcends it.[51]

One of the most common and serious obstacles to modern man in accepting revealed religion proceeds precisely from the fact that he is educated to a progressively restricted form of knowledge and of certitude. It is the so-called scientific method, which limits the human capacity to know to experimental observation and to quantitative reasoning, to physical and to mathematical science. Such methodology results in massive evidence and man therefore finds great satisfaction in it.[49]

He will not tolerate, except wearily, other forms of thought, which seek other truths and other realities by other ways. These truths thus remain unexplored and excluded from the interests of modern man.[49]

He nourishes his spirit, so needful of escaping from the purely mechanical dimensions of positivist thought, on fantastic imaginings or subjective sentiments that have nothing to do with higher reality and nothing to do with the Living God.[49]

Revelation is communicated by way of a tradition, by way of a teaching. It is born in determined, historical moments, and has its roots in personal and concrete elements. But then it becomes doctrine and teaching for all men.[49]

If, then, I add that the acceptance of revelation, that is the faith, is not verified in the human heart except by way of the secret aid of God, without grace, we have added to the picture of revelation its depth, its atmosphere, and its mysterious and immense Spirit.[49]

It pervades and animates all, as indeed it should, because revelation accepted is not only a notion perceived, a knowledge similar to others, but a grace, a principle of supernatural life. It is a circulation of the thought of God in us, it is a divine communication, an act of virtue that prepares us in this life for the beatific knowledge of the future life.[49]

CHRISTIANITY VIEWS THE WORLD:

MAN AND HIS SPIRITUAL DIMENSION

The Christian Predicament

X
THE MEANING
OF CHRISTIANITY

An objection one often hears today is directed by our materialistic age against the Christian who seeks the Kingdom of Heaven. What is contested is the legitimacy of his claim and capacity to seek the kingdom of earth. Should hope for things eternal exclude the hope for temporal well-being? Are the two hopes incompatible? Did not the Master say that no man can serve two masters? [52]

It is a delicate question, and it shapes the torment of our age. On the one side are those who would choose a wholly spiritual solution, challenging the Christian's right to concern himself with temporal things, demanding that he live a life of utopian angelism with certain Manichean overtones. On the other side are those who would have the Christian gather up the benefits of religion with those of the profane world, somewhat as we see done in the Old Testament.[52]

For the Christian the supreme precept of life is love. He has a deep concern for the concrete and human needs of his time, but he flees the totalitarian spirit of those who have no other hope than that founded on the things of this world.[52]

The Christian is by definition a man in whom the moral estimate of life has the highest and most decisive importance. To a Christian, action is worthwhile if it is moral, if it is good. For him everything falls under a moral judgment, everything is classified according to the ultimate categories of good and of evil. Sensitivity to moral nuance does not paralyze but rather guides him, strengthens him and impels him to "action," because moral action is nothing other than the seeking after good—and the good provokes love, and love brings forth life and movement.[9]

Yet when a Christian becomes involved, and expresses either concern or criticism, or a kind of cautious and conditioned approval, or when he expresses his vision of the world in which he lives, he is challenged immediately. He is accused of not being wholly attuned to the nuances of life in the affluent society. He is thrust beyond the pale, as one who cannot possibly understand this state of temporal well-being, which should merit the support of everyone because of the abundance and comfort it creates, because of its very vitality.[14]

The Christian is thus summarily excluded from the decisive moments in which man determines the value and direction his economic and social activity will have.[14]

The Christian's moral stance, it is said, chills every celebration, takes away the joy of liberty, and sows scruples and melancholy wherever he goes.[14]

This is one of the causes of contemporary secularism. The Christian seems to represent a concept contrary to the material progress to which our time owes its strength and beauty. The Christian, confronted with economic progress, is a man of renunciation, of poverty, of flight from the world. He is a cross bearer: how can he claim full citizenship in the world of modern civilization? [14]

It is well for the Christian to think about this, because such an attitude surrounds him with diffidence, isolation and even hostility.[14]

It is of course an objection that makes headway in societies characterized by absolute faith in the primacy of economic factors: the world of classic capitalism and of Marxism. It takes root also among youth, when they do not have a clear understanding of the meaning of life.[14]

Such thinking is so common that I consider it to be one of the most serious and urgent questions of our day: to determine the relationship that should exist between Christian life and modern life, the former understood as faith in the challenge of the Gospels, the latter as that life that is pervaded by the quest for and the attainment of temporal well-being. In other words, what value does the Christian give to the things of this world? [14]

My first observation is that the Christian is a priori an optimist in his consideration of the goods of this earth. He is not hostile; he favors them. He is not scandalized; he admires them. He is not fearful; he is sympathetic towards them.[14]

In this context, there comes to mind the repeated and marvelous and mysterious words of the Bible, which express the admiration of God contemplating the work of His creation: "And God saw that it was good." The Shaper of the universe delights in His own work. God sees Himself reflected in His creatures. He admires their order, movement, grandeur, beauty, and depth. He hears the canticle, which rises from the cosmos created by Him.

He measures the force of His own power and of His own freedom.[14]

This could be for us, too, an overwhelming meditation: to consider almost with the mind of God the very essence of things. Before it we remain confounded. Perhaps this confrontation will be the wellspring of the religious summons to the man of tomorrow which the scientific world of yesterday has lost.[14]

Are not the works of man born of intelligence, of patience, and of toil? Do they not express usefulness and beauty? Then we should acknowledge it because of the development it gives, within the structure of our earthly life, to the work of God. Man plumbs the potentialities of God's creation. He brings them to life, he unveils their marvels, he harnesses their power, he rejoices in their benefits.[14]

The effort by which modern man seeks to know, to dominate and to use nature and to employ it in his service may well be considered a worthy reply to the gift God has made of it to man. The creative voice of God still speaks to us of the meaning of the world: "Fill the earth and make it yours." Nature, therefore, invites us to explore it, to conquer it and to possess it.[14]

But the invitation does not intend to fix man exclusively in the realm of the temporal so much as to move him along the way, or better, up the ladder that brings him back to the point of departure, brings him back to God.[14]

Work and the conquest of the natural world are meant to be only a way that leads man back to the first source of life. It is necessary, therefore, to explore this universe with the religious sense of a divine presence, almost of an encounter with the Divine, which is at once profoundly concealed, and yet profoundly manifest.[14]

But there is a surprise in store for those who go questing: the encounter with the Word of God come upon the stage of the world as man, the encounter with the Incarnation. Our experience of the created world is transformed into an extraordinary adventure, a magnificent revelation. This is how Saint Paul expresses it: "Everything is yours . . . but you are Christ's, and Christ is God's." And he adds: "All that rings true, all that commands reverence, and all that makes for right; all that is pure, all that is lovely, all that is gracious in the telling . . . let this be the argument of your thoughts." [14]

The Christian is not insensible to the world of nature and to its temporal realities; he is not an escapist, he is not a dreamer, he is not absorbed in the angelism of a spiritual world. Rather he is one who can have the highest and noblest perspective on the value of the temporal, and confront it with greater realism and with a capacity to deal effectively with it.[14]

Christianity is not an obstacle to modern progress. This is because it does not consider progress only in its technical and economic aspect, but in the perspective of its total development. Temporal goods can, of course, assist in the full development of man, but they cannot constitute the ideal of human perfection nor the essence of social progress.[14]

The Christian sees in temporal goods the work and the gift of God. He admires them and uses them. He does not make idols of them. He remembers always the first com-

mandment, "You shall have no other God before Me."
And it is here, therefore, that the drama of conflict between the Christian and temporal realities is joined.[14]

From his earliest youth the Christian is reminded that
in the things of this world, especially in the direction given
them by human or diabolical malice, there can be and
there often is a profound and mysterious disorder. Neither
human nature as it is today nor the works it produces are
always good. Evil exists even beyond the control of our
will; we are surrounded by it. All the struggles for human
progress that history records would be meaningless were
this not true.[14]

The Christian is aware also of this aspect of reality. He
is not ingenuous. He is not passive and rather foolishly
optimistic. He divines the tragic element in life and hears
also the groan of creation as it awaits regeneration.[14]

Through the sorcery of modern man, even the forces
of nature can unleash formidable threats and immense destruction. The atom bomb teaches us this.[14]

And thus whoever is wise, whoever is a Christian, cannot but be alarmed by such dangers, which progress itself,
separated from the primacy of higher moral law, brings in
its wake.[14]

What, it may be asked, is the relationship between the
Catholic and the citizen? The question is broad and fundamental because it can locate both in the order of history
and of ideas, the role of Christianity in the life of humanity.[53]

The problem receives sharper dimension when considered in the context of the relationship between Church and
state, and further when it contemplates the role that Catholics play in civil life. The question can assume significant

proportions if it refers to the ultimate and specific ends of the two societies of which a Catholic is a part: the one religious, the other temporal. How should these two ends of man be considered? One is spiritual and other-worldly, the other natural and of this world. Are they necessarily in opposition and hostile to each other? And in every case the question must be asked: How does all this affect the man to whom this double destiny is assigned? [53]

In the very act of affirming this double finality of the eternal and the temporal for man, his true destiny, the reality of his life, is fully reflected. The recurring attempt to deny either the one or the other, or to absorb them in a kind of finalistic monism, can give rise to a kind of temporal theocracy on the one hand, and to a totalitarian laicism on the other.[53]

Should either happen, liberty—in both cases, but in different ways—would be gravely offended; and so, too, would civilization and peace. Christ's famous dual judgment of rendering to God and Caesar has fixed the extreme limits within which human society and true progress can have a free and orderly development.[53]

Must Catholics, therefore, have no share in the life lived in their country? Must they remain passive and indifferent to its developing life, to its necessities, and even to its tragedies? [53]

Should they be considered a kind of dead weight on society, useless and harmful precisely because they profess a religious faith which offers them an inexhaustible supply of spiritual energy and of moral virtues by which they seek to live? [53]

Should they close the door on life and live their religion

as though it were a purely private affair, timid and almost ashamed of having an open and stimulating public and collective expression of that faith? Or should they be considered a group of spiritual initiates, concerned only with their own personal perfection and spiritual enjoyment, cut off from the currents operating in history, when these very currents derive from Christianity whatever about them is beneficial, whether or not this be admitted.[53]

There is no room for instability or tepidity. The Christian cannot stop midway nor abandon himself to opportunistic or unworthy compromises. For the Christian, liberty, of course; but responsibility, too.[107]

No Catholic can be passive, or indifferent, or closed, or egotistical. He cannot be dreamy-eyed, shut off from the reality of his time and from the needs of his brothers. The Catholic should be in the forefront in contributing on the real terrain of modern life.[53]

He should, therefore, cooperate in the building of a new society, one that is sane and brotherly. He should be involved in the true problems of the age, and draw strength from the authentic moral and spiritual forces of the Catholic religion.[53]

To the Catholic I say this: See to it that the principles that you profess and that are drawn from your faith are always meaningful and operative in your life. They are the light and they should never be put out. They are truths to be lived, they are not conceptual abstractions; it is false to believe one protects them by putting them beyond discussion, in order to assume standards of judgment and action which are purely rational or technical.[53]

Faith cannot be separated from life. "The just man," says Saint Paul, that is the man who is the true man, the wise man, the Christian man, "lives by faith." He does not live only with the faith, as if it should be isolated in stagnant compartments, which the practical man of action cannot comprehend. But I repeat—he lives *by faith,* that is, he draws from it the standards of his actions and the strength to carry them out.[53]

The wise and illuminating presence of Christian principles, be sure of this, will not make you lose the clear and concrete perspective of the things of this world, nor will it render less positive and mordant the action which is employed in their cause.[53]

Can there be for each of us in this life an epiphany, a manifestation of God in proportion to our capacity? And looking at the contemporary world this other question immediately comes to mind: Can our age also have its own epiphany, which would correspond to its talents and its capacity? [49]

Let us think for a moment of the Gospel story of the Magi. They moved towards Christ, the center of revelation, led by a star; moved, that is, by the observation of an astronomical, physical, experimental fact. They begin with a scientific study, which does not remain an end in itself but becomes a sign of another more important reality to which they direct not only their minds but also their steps, as trusting and courageous pilgrims.[49]

This story has much to teach us. When the scientific world begins to appreciate its meaning, a new spirit of religion will awaken in contemporary thought. Religious indifference and a sense of proud sufficiency, which are caused by the enormous scientific progress of our time, will no longer halt the impetus of the human spirit by unaccountable concern for secondary causes, but will cre-

128   DIALOGUES

ate in it a religious need that is stronger and more rational,
oriented toward a truer philosophy and a truer religion.[49]

And from an ever more fruitful observation of natural
phenomena it will draw a more logical and comforting
conviction of the marvelous harmony reigning in the universe, which, as Einstein, who did not have a doctrinal
religious perspective, said, "is an essential motive of scientific research." [49]

"The most beautiful thing," Einstein has written, "that
we can experiment with is the mysterious." It is the source
of every true art and science. To recognize that what is
impenetrable to us exists truly, manifesting itself as a
higher wisdom and a more radiant beauty which our
obtuse faculties can understand only in their most primitive forms, is at the center of any true spirit of religion.
This spirit of religion Einstein calls "cosmic religious experience." It is a magnificent preface to natural religion,
a preface in its turn to revelation.[49]

Revelation, I insist, does not of itself oblige. What it
announces is not verified by intrinsic evidence. It demands
"good will," a complex of subjective requirements on the
part of man, which in great part depend on his free will.[49]

Unfortunately, we delude ourselves by thinking that free
is equivalent to capricious, to stubborn, to rebellious. We
do not stop to think how much liberty is the soul of honesty, of the voluntary and direct seeking of the good.[49]

To reach the truth, religious truth above all, it is necessary to be extremely loving of truth. It is necessary to
seek it, to know it, to wait for it, and to preserve it, to
receive it whence and how it comes, to be, in a word,
disciples of it, and to offer to it the homage of a disin-
terested, honest, and coherent thought.[49]

When a society is composed of living men, that is, men living by the grace of God, and living truly as Christians, it can be hoped that in the world's tomorrow there will be no more poor who suffer hunger, no more injustice that has no repair, no more misery without remedy. Christian society will know also how to remove these consequences of sin.[16]

Religion seeks to unite human life with the divine. Perfect religion will be that which annihilates distance and which succeeds in leaping the immense abyss which opens between man and God, God the transcendent, God the mystery, God the eternity, God the infinite. How will man be able to effect this? How will he be able to unite himself to God? What will be the bridge? [17]

It is Christianity that constitutes the bridge. "He descended from heaven and became flesh." The Lord calls us, He wishes to talk with us and at the end He says to us: I desire that your life may become immersed in Mine as a drop of water in the ocean. We must become dissolved in Christ, and in order that this may happen, Christ wishes our life to be incorporated into His.[17]

The Christian life rests precisely on the principle of a vital communication made by God to us. Religion is no longer a distance between man and God. It is no more fear of divinity, it is not only a colloquy, it is a "communicatio," a sharing of the life of God, a becoming a consort of the divine nature. It is being associated in some way with the divine nature. But this association, this participation in God, is neither sensible, nor experimental.[54]

The divine message becomes even more eloquent and fascinating today now that the kingdoms of space are open to conquest by the genius and boldness of man. And yet how is it that when the first Sputnik was launched an intelligent poet could think that it was a victory of atheism rather than an invitation to contemplate more fully that universe that sings the glory of God? [41]

Will it not happen perhaps to modern man as slowly his scientific studies progress and laws and realities buried in the mute face of matter come to be discovered, that he will hear the marvelous voice of the spirit vibrating within it? Will this be the religion of tomorrow? [41]

Or will it not be perhaps my religion of today that already speaks to me, to the point of flooding my spirit and of making it spill over with stupor and with joy, in the infinite power and infinite wisdom of the God Whom I adore, Whom I love, of the God Who is living and true? [41]

As a vision of the truths it presents and of the relationships it creates, religion ranges over the whole panorama of life and touches the horizon of reality. It does not merely trace particular relationships, it describes the complete arc of the general order of relationships. Nothing is extraneous to it, nothing is superior to it. Everything enters into the universal conception that it proposes.[41]

Those who limit the sector of their observation and of their experience, as do so many scholars and men of affairs, do not understand this universal claim of religion.[41]

The universality that follows on the mystery of the Incarnation and bases its relationships between men on their relationship with Christ and God is wholly contrary to totalitarianism, to the negation, that is, of the human personality, and to the throttling of the legitimate expansion of the liberty of each and every man.[39]

This is especially true in the religious sphere in which it has its foundation and its first affirmation. Christian universality, that is catholicity, does not oppose the multiplicity of kingdoms of this world nor its various sovereignties and temporal authorities.[39]

Those who believe that Christianity, because it is founded on immutable dogmas and governed by a fixed and unalterable authority, tends to crystallize a given social order or disorder, and is by its very nature socially conservative, do not have an exact idea of Christianity.[55]

They do not make a distinction between what is firm and eternal and stable in its juridical and historical evolution and what is instead capable of change, moving constantly from a present, concrete and human expression toward a new and superior expression, which better responds to its goal of saving man, of regenerating him interiorly and socially.[55]

The order to which Christianity tends is not static but an order in continual evolution toward a higher form; it is equilibrium in motion. Founded on absolute principles, it profits from all of the contingencies that history renders relative to it in order to give unceasing proof of its salvific and transforming vitality.[55]

Christianity does not fear renewal on any level of human life. It wishes it and inspires it where an ever greater justice is desirable and a more faithful type of humanity is realizable. In arousing the concept and the desire of spiritual renovation in the hearts of men, it prepares the peaceful and ennobling path also for their social renovation.[55]

Christianity is not a puritanical religion that holds itself aloof from the world, that tends to conserve itself by abstaining from the real conditions in which humanity lives. It is made for humanity, it is the religion of humanity, and its mission is to penetrate the social fabric and the conscience of each man in order to renovate and vivify it.[55]

Christianity has something infinitely precious to offer those who are not yet Christian. These are its "principles," that is, its fundamental ideas on life; the general conception it has of the world, the *Weltanschauung,* which has been the very soul of our civilization, and which is today so forgotten and so repudiated.[55]

Christianity is the light of the world, it is the strength of the spirit, it is the leaven of mankind. Christianity has the talent of reform and of newness no less than that of tradition and of fidelity because it has the secret of life.[55]

Christianity is always coherent in itself but is never satisfied with itself. It is not for this reason either restless or subversive. Christianity, alert to the continual reform of itself and of the world, is never deluded but optimistic; it is not for this reason lazy or egotistical. Its hunger and its thirst for justice form one of its "beatitudes" because it knows what justice is and where and how it ought to be sought.[55]

The secret of life and the consciousness of justice have been revealed to Christianity by its founder and master, Christ the Lord. By His resurrection He has added to this revelation the grace of attaining it. It is to Christianity, therefore, rather than to other schools of thought and to other principles, that our world should look, for the guidance and strength necessary to effect its own moral and social renovation.[55]

Today one hears so much talk about giving to the world

a "human" face, but often what is intended is a face deprived of a human soul, materialized by the fallacious hope of drawing from the earth whatever is necessary to make man a happy and complete person. This way of thinking assumes that the solution of economic problems, the technical organization of human labor, the scientific exploration of nature, can liberate and redeem man, and that human effort, having gained mastery over the sensible world, can by itself attain its true destiny.[56]

In the mentality of many men of our time, even Christians, occupied in giving to temporal things a higher purpose, it is insinuated that this is indeed the greatest and perhaps the only effective duty to fulfill. It follows then that it is Christianity that should advance the goals of this world rather than that the world should serve the true ends of man destined to a supernatural order.[56]

The order of redemption, of grace and of eternal life seems to this way of thinking to be an elective and indifferent superstructure, irrelevant to the practical conduct of individual and social life. The idea of a naturalistic messianism is thus created. The more fully this idea is realized the more it shows itself to have increased, and not satisfied, the profound needs of human life, and to have created not a new humanity but a new era of temporal and illusory materialism.[57]

The Christian life is a reality always in the process of becoming. It is a reality in part already attained, in part yet to be attained. It is a reality that in certain aspects is luminous and joyful and in certain others weighty, enigmatic, and mysterious. Saint Paul says it clearly: "Our knowledge, our prophecy, are only glimpses of the truth." We are already on the way of salvation, but "although we have already begun to reap our spiritual harvest, we groan in our hearts, waiting for that adoption which is the ransoming of our bodies from their slavery." [57]

The Christian life is bound to its future destiny, which Christ in rising from the dead has revealed and has also attained for us. The Christian life under one aspect is wholly fed by a memory of the first coming of Christ and by the memory of the Gospel and of the virtue drawn from it.[57]

Under another aspect it is wholly projected toward the future, a future that transcends the historical horizon and that expresses itself in its eschatological destiny, the ultimate and final end of humanity. The Kingdom of Heaven to which Christian messianism tends begins here and now, in time, but it is manifested and it completes itself in the future, there where Christ awaits us and calls us.[57]

The Christian life, therefore, bound as it is to Christ Who has arisen, is governed by an ascetic and moral complex that looks beyond the sphere of temporal interests. The complex is characterized by a double effect: of a relative detachment from the things of earth, and of a living hope of what is promised for the future life. The Christian life can, with another purpose, make its own the formula of Stoic wisdom; *abstine et sustine*.[57]

The call to a different, superior and future life can seem to us distracting and unreal. We live fascinated by the illusion of the present life. Indeed many of those who profess the Christian ideal are often more attuned to the conquest and attainment of economic and temporal progress than they are to the defense of the moral values of the Christian life.[57]

They often do not know how to derive from the light

of their principles the norms and the energies to give this world an order that better mirrors Christian principles. Nor do they know how to subordinate temporal interests to the primacy of the spiritual life and of justice determined by the supreme purpose of our life.[57]

The present life is a delusion for whoever places his supreme hopes in it. It is measured by time, which means to say that our mortal life will have in time, in which we place our total trust, its inexorable end. The present life is governed by values that are not enough to satisfy the immense and limitless capacity of desiring and of enjoying that man possesses. It is cut short by death, the great enemy, which laughs at the man who has not prepared himself to overcome it for the moment of his final triumph.[57]

Christianity will be pessimistic, if you wish to use the word, because of the sincere and fundamental knowledge it has of evil, because of the realistic cures that it applies to it, because of the humble and patient experience it has of human misery.[58]

But it will be optimistic at the same time because it proclaims that suffering is not definitive, not useless, not despairing; that it is productive also of moral elevation and of merit, and that evil is not invincible. And since the Christian already lives a kind of mystical experience of good, of the supreme good already attained, if still not fully enjoyed, he dares to make his own the marvelous exclamation of Saint Paul: "I cannot contain myself for happiness in the midst of all these trials of mine!" [58]

Christ is for all. For all men, for all times, for all nations. He came for the world. The earth, therefore, is for Him. History is for Him.[58]

This truth is extraordinary indeed. It is magnificently modern, it is marvelously productive. The profoundly merciful thought of God says that He excludes no one from His plan of goodness and salvation. It is in this idea of universal mercy that we know God better than in the knowledge that we have of His other works and of the world.[58]

The universality of Christianity bespeaks the dimension of the love of God and the largeness of the heart of Christ.[57]

It says also how a destiny of unity penetrates human history. It brings humanity together as brothers, and makes the barriers of human antagonism fall. It inaugurates a "becoming" of peace. It calls every racial, ethnic, national and cultural expression to take part, each with its own dignity, in the great concert of spiritual and civil harmony, which is proper to Christianity.[57]

XI

THE MINISTRY OF THE CHURCH

To what end does my ministry tend? I will tell you: to your consolation. I am here in your midst, the survivor of a tradition which you are forgetting and abandoning, a herald always of ancient words, which remain ever the same and ever mysterious.[19]

You indeed move and make progress daily. You create a new mentality, you express a new form of life, which is profane and modern and wholly attuned to earthly realities. Exhilarated by the experience that follows contact with the things of this world, you believe yourselves thus to be assured, modern, and also even to be happy.[19]

But you are not happy. The reason is that you habitually seek what does not exhaust your capacity for desiring, for thinking, and for rejoicing. The knowledge of purpose is diminished in you, the supreme reason of things and of life escapes you.[19]

Perhaps this does not even bother you. You are saturated with the "means" of life and you are often lacking in understanding and capacity to decide what purpose all of these should finally serve. You work hard and exhaust yourselves and oftentimes you do not understand the why

137

of it all. Therefore there comes a time when you seek comfort, you seek reassurance, you seek a confirmation that all of your activity is not in vain and that your road does indeed wind purposively.[19]

You have need of hearing words of the spirit that can justify your weariness, that can redirect your feelings, that can comfort your delusions and console your sufferings. You have need of spiritual integration, of a moral complement that can give your life a sense of human and superhuman fulness.[19]

Perhaps I do not know how to give this consolation and this fulness to you. My voice is weak and my actions inept, my example insignificant and my love lacking. Forgive me if my ministry is ineffective. But do not look at my poor labors, do not stop only when you hear my voice. Hear the voice of which I am but a weak echo. Look at the work of which I am only a herald and an instrument.[19]

The voice—you hear it—is the good news. The work—think of it—is your salvation. This is the Gospel: "I bring you tidings of great joy." This is the voice of Christmas resounding in the prophetic night of Bethlehem, and its echo is not spent. It spreads still throughout the world, it transcends history, it overcomes the centuries, it ploughs through space, it hovers over mankind and it reaches finally into the conscience of man. There is a happy announcement, there is a blessed announcement. For each and every one, there is a message of truth, a message of goodness.[19]

Christ is the consolation, Christ is the happiness, Christ is the richness of the world. He is the prophet of beatitude. I would wish that each of you could feel once again as something new, discover with wonder the words of interior liberty and of strength that proclaim the coming of the Saviour, because Saviour is His name.[19]

The Christ who has come for all, the Christ who opens to those who are least fortunate the blessing of His salvation, this blessed Christ will be possessed by whoever wishes to possess Him.[48]

His salvation will not be given to us without our co-operation. It is not magic, it is not automatic, nor is it an inevitable predestination nor a gift imposed on one who does not wish to receive it. The economy of the un-merited and overwhelming mercy of God does not dispense us from cooperation, which should be personal, proceeding from our good will, at least from a conditional commitment of acceptance.[48]

Thus the coming of Christ among us brings sharply into focus, as a crisis and fatal choice, the vocation of liberty in the scheme of our salvation. Called to a supernatural destiny, we are free, we are responsible for the choices by which we apply this destiny to ourselves, or by the way in which we reject it. The moral drama of the world and of souls thus becomes tremendous and grandiose.[48]

God by His very nature, by His infinite transcendence, is inaccessible, incomprehensible and ineffable. Our seeking after Him ends in mystery. It is not a mystery deprived of certitude and of joy but rather a mystery which in challenging thought always remains infinitely superior to it.[47]

Man with respect to God lives in a continuous drama, that of being made for Him, of having need of Him and of being tormented by the quest for Him, and not being able ever adequately to find Him. Man will always be aware of his own blindness as gradually God reveals Himself to him as knowable. He will always be more conscious of being able to love God than to know God, and of his duty of desiring Him more than of finding Him.[47]

God is at the same time knowable and ineffable, light and mystery. This is perhaps the explanation of, but not the justification for, the fact that a great part of mankind is passive and bewildered before the problem of God. Men do not know how to seek Him as they should nor to pray to Him nor to direct their lives to Him. Often they have tired of the difficult climb toward this transcendent goal and have stopped along the way to create idols for themselves, or to feed themselves on the illusion of being able to do without God. Or else in contemplating themselves, they have mistaken the vestiges of God that they find reflected in their human spirit for the great Sun that He alone is.[47]

Our relationship to God appears in all that we are, in all that we do at every moment of our lives. Our dependence on His creative action and His loving Providence emerges vividly in the Gospels. From this point of view there is nothing that is not sacred, because nothing exists of itself and for itself.[8]

From this it is easy to see the importance of doctrine in determining the fate of humanity. We clearly see how blessed we are by the coming of Jesus Christ into the world. He came to forge a unique link between humanity and God.[25]

This religious link, respecting and ennobling the human person, is the most solid and hopeful basis for unity between men. The true sociology of human peace takes its rise from Christian religious unity. It is this unity, introduced by Christ into human thought and history, that we so earnestly desire.[25]

It is to Christ, then, that we offer the profession of our faith. We make our own the expression of that faith that Peter addressed to Him: "You are the Christ, the Son of the living God." And we say to Him, with Peter: "Lord, to whom shall we go? You alone have the words of eternal life." And again we make our own Peter's cry of sorrow and sincere avowal: "Lord, You know everything; You know that we love You." [40]

If God willed the Incarnation, the assuming of human flesh by the divine, and if He willed the Redemption, the great drama of the Passion and of the expiating death of Christ, it is a sign that God has chosen and refined the human setting of our life and of our history. [59]

History has become the theater of His revelation and of His communication with man. [59]

The Church, which is nothing if it is not the continuation of Christ in time, is the point of encounter between God and man. [59]

God fixed no point of encounter other than a human one, in Christ. This point of encounter is not individual and single for each man, but one that is social and organized. It is the Church, where each man can find Christ and communicate with Him. [59]

In His wisdom, God has wished that each of us receive the gifts of His love through the community. [59]

This may be because it is only the community that can realize the total range of possible human and Christian greatness, and because any isolation is an impoverishment and a weakness. This happens both on the human and supernatural level, which is the level of the paternal love of God. [59]

He loves me, and He loves each of us individually. But

He has also wished that each of us should gain union with Him through the union that exists between ourselves and our brothers.[59]

This, simply, is why the Church exists.[59]

The Christian mission is original. It is demanding. It is easier to live it than to define it. The mission of the Church consists in extending in the world the life of Christ, and in helping humanity participate in His mysteries: the Incarnation and Redemption.[60]

The mission of the Church therefore is to establish a communion of life with Christ, with a resulting communion of brotherhood with man, centered in Him.[60]

The mission of the Church is to generate the Church, to make it live, to spread it, to make it bring forth fruit through the activity of faith, of grace and of the Gospel. Like a living tree, the Church produces itself, sends forth its branches and matures its fruit.[60]

The Christian message is not the simple announcement of some principles that the philosophical development of human thought could as well enunciate. It is not a vague spiritualism seeking to inebriate the emotive capacity of conscience or to deaden the pain of suffering. It is not a lyric prophetism, or a charismatic mysticism, summoning forth hidden and superstitious energies from the interior depths of the imagination and of the instincts.[60]

It is not a naturalistic humanism that tends directly to benefit the temporal order. Nor is it a revolution that seeks to apply justice to social abuse and to raise one class against the other. And, finally, it is not an apathetic resignation to the world as it is, in expectation of future and healing rebirth.[60]

It is the execution of the design of God. It is the object of the prayer of Christ.[60]

Christ is our teacher. The Church will speak, will teach, will repeat His words. Its mission will be to preserve, interpret and proclaim the doctrine of Christ.[60]

Christ lived among men. He is the prototype, the model of the art of living, the example. The imitation of Christ will be the path of the new ethics, the paradigm of restored human virtue, the stairway of asceticism and of heroism.[60]

The sacramental life of the Church constitutes its vital mission, its treasure, which it will renew and communicate.[60]

And to whom will it be communicated? To its children. And where are they? In the world. Therefore the Church comes into contact and enters into a dialogue with the world.[60]

This meeting of the Church with the world presents a drama as complex as it is interesting, mysterious yes, but realistic too. It is the true drama of history. The perspective widens; heavenly and infernal powers meet on the human battleground and in a combat, which is transcendent, and which Providence will direct to its final epilogue.[60]

The Church has a twofold aspect: the first is one of identity, of conservation, of coherence, of community of life, of fidelity, and of presence. This is the Church symbolized in the stability of the rock.[60]

The second aspect is one of movement, of communication, of projection into time and space, of expansion, of dynamism, of eschatological hope. This is the Church symbolized in the moving, living and growing body of Christ.[60]

The history of the Church invites us to consider the trajectory of Christ through the centuries, a trajectory that creates its own history: a history that has meaning and value which it communicates to human history, which does not know where else to seek and find them.[60]

The word "mission," which indicates the immense field which the doctrine of the Church reaches, recalls to mind this figure of movement that so characterizes the life of the Church.[60]

It begins with Christ. The Church is sent by Him, motivated by Him, followed by Him. The Church carries Him within itself, preaches Him, communicates Him and transmits Him. Through the Church, Christ reaches man. He vaults the confines of nations, transcends the centuries, and comes in contact with human life, its forms, its institutions, its customs, its civilization.[60]

The Church undergoes obstacles, rebuff, persecution. Through the centuries it moves, suffering and sorrowing, praying and working, teaching and blessing. It moves toward a goal, which draws it, as though it were near.[60]

Sustained by this vision, the Church is unaware of fatigue or of delusion. It runs, in the hope of that final day in which the mysterious Christ it bears within itself will reveal Himself and absorb and beatify it in Himself. This is eternal life.[60]

The problem of the contacts between the mission of the Church and the world is a problem that is always open. It is because the world, especially today, is in a phase of profound and rapid evolution, and because the application and announcing of the Christian good news admits of a variety of times and forms.[60]

It seems to me that this relationship of the Church to the world, without precluding other legitimate forms of expression, can be represented best in a dialogue. This has been suggested by the custom, by now widespread, of conceiving the relationship between the sacred and the secular in terms of the transforming dynamism of modern society and of the pluralism of its manifestations. It is expressed, too, in terms of the maturity of man, be he religious or not, enabled through secular education to speak and to act through the dignity of dialogue.[115]

The distinction between the sacred and the profane merits a particular and attentive study. The problem lends itself to harmful misunderstandings and can receive mistaken solutions. An absolute separation of the sacred from the profane can wholly paralyze or neutralize the mission of the Church. Modern secularism, which uses an apparent reverence for the sacred in order to exclude it from the area of real life, knows it well.[60]

But it is certain that the mission of the Church is to bring the sacred into a determined relationship with the profane in such a way that the sacred is not contaminated but communicated, and the profane is not altered but sanctified. It is the mystery of the Incarnation of God-made man that is here continued. It is easy to speak of it, but difficult to implement.[60]

The Church is not only a visible society with religious aims. The Church is a mystery. Its head is Christ, Who lived twenty centuries ago, but Who lives also today, because of His resurrection.[59]

He has no successors, He has only visible representatives.[59]

The question may be asked here: Are there two heads of the Church? The answer is an easy one. The true and supreme head of the Church, the only source of its salvation, is Christ, the Lord. The Pope, successor of St. Peter is the head of the Church also, but subordinated to and wholly deriving from Christ.[118]

It is the strength, the holiness and the truth of the Father that animate the Church. It is always through the Church and in relationship to it that Christ, the God-Man, manifests His action and communicates the life of the Father to all mankind.[59]

Meditation upon the profound reality of the Church reveals an initial vision of the Church as the continuation of Christ. It is "His Church," the sphere of His action, the "place" where He acts through the Holy Spirit.[59]

Christ does not abandon his own. He returns to communicate to them His life, His doctrine, His redemption, and to prepare them for their meeting with the Father.[59]

In the Church we find ourselves in the house of our Father. We are flanked and supported by our brothers. And most especially, we find the Mother of God, Mary most holy.[59]

She is not only a beautiful historical figure who has given us Jesus, once and for all, in time. She continually affects the spiritual development of her children, as a mother affects the child still within her womb. Without Mary, the Church could appear to us as cold and impersonal. But instead she is present, the Mother who knows and loves us, and who is not aloof from the intimate drama of the least of her children.[59]

For the glory, therefore, of the Virgin Mary and for our own consolation, I proclaim Mary Mother of the Church, that is of the whole people of God, of the faithful and of their pastors. I desire that through this title the Mother of God should be still more honored and invoked by the entire Christian people.[119]

Unity is the essential and distinctive note of the Church of Christ. It is necessary for the Christian religion.[61]

The unity of the Church is not pure uniformity of doctrine. It is not, as was said of Calvin's Geneva, "a bibliocracy." It is no mere disciplinary submission to a hypothetically uniform code of beliefs and practices; it is not even belonging to a community of the faithful organized into a compact and homogeneous association that calls itself by the sacred name of Church.[61]

It is not the sum of diverse and divided bodies bound together by some imprecise ecumenical chain. Even as it is not merely the result of a religious society that was governed by a college of bishops, or a group of patriarchs, that is by a hierarchy without a head.[61]

It is the form—that is, the note and quality, beauty and life, the mystery—of the people of God, gathered into a visible and religious society, under the direction of the bishops, with the Bishop of Rome, the universal Bishop, the Pope, as its head.[61]

But how did this nascent community of love become the community of authority? Did the power that governs it grow out of the community itself? Or did the authority precede the community, convoke it, create it, sanctify it, and direct it? [61]

It is the history of the Church that shows unequivocally that it is the hierarchy that is the apostle, the missionary that evangelizes humanity, draws the faithful from it and places them in a living church. It is not an amorphous and arbitrary community of the faithful, which chooses from its midst the pastor who should guide it.[61]

The concept of the one church should never be for us a purely historical and juridical one, referring only to those who compose it and to the visible face of the Church. It should be understood also in its relationship to Christ and to God, as an intrinsic principle of that reality that makes of the Church a mystery—that is, a thought, a plan, a work of God.[61]

The Church was one in the design of God even before its historical realization, which Christ began in the Gospel and which continues to develop in time what will be fulfilled beyond time.[61]

Unity involves two consequences: one is exclusivity, the other is obedience.[61]

Unity is not promiscuity, it is not multiplicity. Unity, in the very act of affirming and determining itself, also distinguishes and defines itself. Unity divides those who belong from those who do not. Catholic unity therefore appears as a concept, indeed an exclusive program, of the religious life. For this reason Christ said that He had come not to bring peace but the sword.[61]

The fear of offering obedience to an arbitrary and tyrannical power is absolutely without foundation. Obedience certainly involves humility and patience and sacrifice. But it is not unreasonable if it is wished by Christ. It is in any case not without limits if confined to a determined competence. It is not foreign to the good of those who profess it; indeed it guarantees and defends that good.[61]

Union with Rome, loyalty to the Vicar of Christ, is not servitude, but brotherhood. It is derived directly from the traditions of the Apostles. For Peter, though indeed their Prince, referred to himself as their brother, and taught that government in the Church should not be by constraint, but by love; not by lording it over one's charges, but by becoming, in mind and heart, their example.[112]

The Church presents two faces to the world: the one, exterior, can appear exhausted and stained by time and by the world; the other, interior, is holy and sanctifying. The first is human and therefore susceptible to defect and anguish. The other is divine and radiant.[59]

The man who sees the Church only from the outside will suffer from time to time from its human imperfections, although an impartial eye should be able to discover much that is admirable even in the temporal aspect of this vessel of salvation.[59]

But he who enters into its life will weep with joy, seeing the Church as the beautiful spouse of Christ. In the Church humanity is transfigured; it becomes mother, teacher and saint. The man who enters will rejoice to discover that it has been waiting for him, and has reserved a place for him, as one not filled at table, as one prepared for a son absent for a time who, in returning, seeks and finds happiness.[59]

Too many see the Church only in its external manifestations: its organization, the coherence of its doctrine and of its moral life, the evidence of perfection and of sanctity in those who accept it completely. They note also its impressive twenty centuries of history, its survival in spite of the sins of its members, and finally, its hierarchy, its charity, and the revolutionary impact of its influence in the world and on civilization.[59]

The literature of the last century amused itself with the almost obligatory theme of the priest inferior to his mission, who, without consciously willing to depart from his vocation, so poorly incarnated and served it as to inflict on it the alternate ignominy, that of ridicule.[62]

Today, literature, when it speaks of the priest and the believer, has an entirely different motive. It idealizes the man who is in the Church, presents him as he ought to be, and in its way makes us realize how that which is real is inferior to the ideal.[62]

Almost without wishing it, it creates a diffidence of attitude toward the Christian in real life who appears to be deceptive and empty of what could justly be sought in him: an interior life, magnanimity, heroism, humility, disinterest, love. And when the author or modern artist exalts some quality, he seems to have the cleverness to suggest that this quality or merit is not properly religious and is not one of the characteristics of the catholic life—clerical life, they would say.[62]

The awareness of the disproportion between the Church as it humanly appears and as it should be is a continuous and searing pain for him who loves the Church and who has some responsibility in it.[62]

Often I experience pain and true suffering when I observe that it is we men of the Church who often offer pretexts and reasons for the world's aversion to the Church and to religion. It is oftentimes a world deprived of culture, and quick to judge summarily the spiritual values of the Church from the manner in which the clergy and the faithful personify them.[62]

This aversion is found also in cultivated people, who by instinct want to find in men and circumstances which qualify as religious a representation worthy of so demanding a profession. They are often instead scandalized by seeing a sight profoundly inferior to what the Christian reality should be.[62]

I feel it my duty to ask forgiveness of so many who have become irritated and incredulous, who are far from God, or Christ, and hostile to the Church because we men of the Church have not given them a worthy example of the ideal that defines us, and we have not known how to merit their esteem and their trust.[62]

Instead of being a way to the truth of the faith and a mirror of Christian virtues, it could be that I have become for men an opaque screen and a severe obstacle.[63]

This is my fault! [62]

Contemporary thinkers have seen the phenomenon of estrangement from religion on a large scale. Modern apostasy numbers among its causes a profound resentment against a Christian world inferior to its principles, "and not only against the Christian world, but against Christianity itself." [62]

Indeed, I will have to consider humbly and seriously this responsibility. I will not blush to ask pardon of the men of my time if I know how to give them neither the intuitive and living image of the reality of the Church, nor the treasure of truth of which it has made me a teacher, nor some experience of its virtue and of its grace, of which I have been made a minister.[62]

Often, those who claim to be scandalized are not. The standard reply to this formidable and recurring objection against the Church is still valid and still worthy of use by the intelligent; that is, to distinguish the person from the office he exercises, the minister from the ministry.[62]

And such an intellectual distinction should not be hard

to make, seeing that we are obliged to practice it every day in social and business life. If it is more difficult to apply it in the religious field—because he who preaches sanctity should be holy, and he who preaches Christ should be authentically Christian—it is not, however, a distinction without application. The validity of supernatural gifts does not depend on those who distribute them, but only on Christ.[62]

There is a kind of antipathy toward the Church that grows in men's minds because the Church is accused of being an old institution. It belongs, they say, to other times. It has had its day. It is, besides, tremendously conservative.[62]

The Church's scrupulous fidelity to the past, they contend, is a chain around the neck of those who remain in the Church, and even those who have left it still feel it binding them.[62]

Tradition is inconceivable for times that have been born of revolution, out of a repudiation of the past and of its so-called useless heritage.[62]

Modern man looks to the present and to the future, not to the past as the Church does and is obliged to do. Thus, for him, the persistence of such a Church in our day is a form of obscurantism and of immobilism.[62]

From all of this arises the impulse of the modern mind to bypass the Church by using its intellectual faculties in the positive and natural sciences, with their technical and industrial orientation of human activity. It seeks to identify with the antireligious eruptions of some contemporary social and political movements, it scorns speculative thought, flees metaphysical reality, and is doubtful about every logical certainty.[62]

Those who still have some regard for the human expressions of past times would reduce the Church to a simple historical phenomenon, a moment in the evolution of civilization, a respectable relic fit for tracts written about mythology or archeology—a museum piece.[62]

They would have for it the benevolence that they have for the dead. For it—the living Church! [62]

I have two observations to make of this way of judging the Church, as if it had the ravages of inexorable old age on its human face or the cadaver-like pallor of an unwelcome ghost.[62]

First: no such judgment of the Church would be made if a true sense of history, wise and informed, were had.[62]

To classify the tradition that the Church preserves and represents as a dead weight on the modern spirit does no honor to our culture, and leaves us incapable of constructing a new civilization that will be stable, coherent, and congenial.[62]

And it is wholly unsubstantiated opinion to consider the Church a mere relic of the past, a creation of time that will be conquered by time. It is a falsehood to call it a Church that looks to its past and counts the centuries as its only glory.[62]

It is true that the Church's eyes are fixed on its source, Christ and His Gospel. It is involved in time and in history. It remembers the fact and the moment that was the redemptive mission of the God-Man in the world.[62]

But it is at the same time turned toward the future. It awaits the future return of Christ in glory. It moves toward its eschatological destiny. It lives from the past but into the present and for the future—and hope is its strength.[62]

Many moderns do not discover in the Church any face

other than one that is frozen and immobile, one made of marble, without movement and without speech. And this is precisely because of the aspect it claims for itself, that of teacher of a dogmatic doctrine, a doctrine that our century calls a prioristic, incomprehensible, beyond discussion and unmoving.[62]

The repugnance for what is called ecclesiastical dogmatism polarizes the lay perspective. The doctrinal intransigence of the Church will end, it is said, in its exclusion from the world of thought, of the schools, of science, and of progress.[62]

This is an old and debated question, complex and delicate, but not without a positive solution. Without going into what is really more meaningful, namely, that dogmas are not arbitrary and dead concepts but living truths, we may rather ask if the Church as a teacher is indeed an obstacle to culture, to thought, to study, and to science? [62]

The facts say no. Today, indeed, it seems that the defense of the validity of thought and the passion for humanistic learning and the most fervent forms of homage to scientific research proceed from the catholic mind in its finest expression. In the midst of modern culture it seeks to sustain a conscience, a faith, an awareness which is menaced on all sides by the materialistic and existentialist currents of our day.[62]

Of the many evils that once afflicted the Church, what can we say? Can we deny them? Can we pass over their gravity? Can we justify them? No! We must be sincere and face reality, historical reality especially, on which a true and more objective evaluation can be made. We should never, in any way, alter it out of love for the Church! [62]

I can affirm that the first to recognize and condemn the failings of the Church has been the Church itself. It has never pretended to be perfect in this world. It accuses itself of every failing it has. It preaches penance to itself, and promotes within itself a continuous reform.[62]

But how, it can be asked, how can the aspect of the Church be so ambiguous, so incomprehensible? Why is it so easy for the Church to be what in truth it is not? [62]

Because it is composed of men. "The Kingdom of Heaven," said Jesus, "is like to a net cast into the sea and which has caught every kind of fish." Thus the good and the bad, the pure and impure, ancients and moderns, barbarians and Greeks—all enter in.[62]

The Church has a soul. That is to say, the Church is a mystery. It is a truth of the faith, and the faith in its intimate and first scintilla of being is grace, the favor of God.[62]

There will never be concerning the Church a tranquillity of opinion and of attitude, and this reminds us not to lose heart if we see the Church not understood, harshly judged and badly treated.[62]

Our sailing, to keep to the lovely image of the apostolic ship so often used, has for its mission to resolve a double problem: to conserve the precious cargo of our religious heritage and to move forward in the choppy sea of this world. To keep afloat and to navigate—such are the simultaneous tasks of the Roman Church, which, in the double symbol of the rock and the ship, expresses magnificently the logic of its duties and its destinies.[63]

Who does not know that the sea of present history is swollen by wind and storms? That our century is in full and dangerous transformation? We must, of course, pray to our divine Master Who sails with us and Who seems strangely asleep, while within us grows the torment of genuine uncertainty and of the imminent danger of foundering, though He will not let us perish.[63]

But, in order not to deserve the reproach He made to His disciples before abating the storm, of being men of little faith, should we not pray to Him to give us greater faith? Should we not pray at the same time that He make us more capable on the one hand of defending the sacred trust we bear with us, and on the other hand of confronting the sea that surrounds us? Of recognizing the historical moment in which we are living, of drawing closer to the unbelieving but noble world in whose midst we live? [63]

One pleasing phenomenon of our time is the Church's spirit of "adaptation" to the thought, manners, trends, and language of the men of our time. This is the "relativism" of the Church, which simply in order to be catholic, reveals, almost daily, new attitudes of acceptance, absorption, purification and even sanctification of the most diverse forms of human life.[82]

May I call to your attention the well-known desire of the Church to facilitate the acceptance of the Gospel by the world. The Church is the first to remove obstacles; its desire is to make smooth the path. It is ever ready to enter into conversation with others. It does not adopt closed and impenetrable positions, nor use words of threat and of anathema, and it is not smug indifference that separates it from a world which does not understand it or desire its presence. Apostolic charity is the very law of its being.[82]

The Church cannot, however, deny or minimize the

truth, whose total content must be protected and communicated, in order to accommodate it to other Christian groups. It cannot betray its faith. It cannot equivocate, using reticence and ambiguity, which would radically deny its mission of fidelity to divine revelation. It cannot, without betraying Christ and denying itself, be content with approximate formula and with random eclecticism.[82]

For us moderns, accustomed as we are to the confused diversity of the philosophical world and to the enduring contradictions of social life, it is difficult to appreciate this doctrinal firmness of the Church. But we should remember that this is for the Church the very reason of its existence, and for the world, the way of its salvation.[82]

Divergencies reflect not merely the state of mind of the protagonists, but the intrinsic complexity of the question. Unity and catholicity, antiquity and modernity, permanence and development, interior values and exterior transactions, a quest for essentials and a care for detail, a vision of things in their roots or in their ramifications: these are the antitheses which make discussion complex and lively because of the very honesty and integrity of the disputants. We await the manifestation of truth with respect, confidence and prayer.[72]

Truth is salvation. Truth is the supreme good. Truth is being, life, God. Truth is therefore the gift of the Church to the world. This is the Church's charity: the higher the truth, the more indispensable is the Church's role in communicating it.[82]

Thus when the Church affirms one of its truths it performs an act of love. If men choose to reject the Church because of this affirmation it cannot be silent, it cannot diminish, it cannot mutilate the truth. This is the drama and often the tragedy of the Word Who came into the world, "His own received Him not." [82]

Today I express this wish for myself and for my collaborators: that we may have as deep and clairvoyant and loving a knowledge as possible of our times in order to overcome its hazards, to take advantage of its possibilities, to discover its sufferings and to reveal its hidden virtues.[63]

Establishing this rapport between the immovable element of faith and the extremely variable times in which we live is a difficult art, a wisdom that requires divine light, a charity that presupposes a detachment from all that is not of real interest to the Kingdom of God.[63]

Thus we will strive to love those who are near and those who are far from us. We will love our own country, and we will love the homeland of others. We will love our friends, we will love our enemies. We will love Catholics, the Orthodox, Protestants, Anglicans, Mohammedans, the indifferent, pagans and atheists.[60]

We will love all social classes, but especially those most in need of assistance. We will love children, and we will love the old, the poor and the sick. We will love those who mock us, who scorn us, who oppose us, who persecute us. We will love those who merit and those who do not merit being loved. We will love our opponents: we will want no man to be our enemy.[60]

We will love the time in which we live: our culture, our science, our art, our sport, our world. We will love, trying to understand, to have sympathy, to admire, to serve and to suffer. We will love with the heart of Christ.[60]

XII

PRAYER

CHRISTIAN PRAYER is a theme as vast as the sea. But the principal form and the one most useful for us is the prayer of the Christian people, considered as a living community and gathered to pay God the tribute of public worship.[64]

The outward form of our religion must express the inner reality. Our spiritual life must be deepened with new inwardness and new conversation with God. Our religious sense, awakened by the wealth of supernatural truths which our faith possesses, must find its own language, one that is lucid and sincere, strong and authentic, full of truth and of poetry, that we may enter into communication with the ever-present God.[64]

The liturgy stands today as a central problem of pastoral life.[64]

Liturgical prayer must give the Church deeper and more genuine knowledge of itself. It must make the Church more lovable and make it easier for it to attract souls to the happiness of a new life with God.[64]

There are still those who consider the liturgical renewal an optional matter, or one of the numerous devotional currents to which a person may give himself or not as he chooses.[64]

Doubtless our spiritual life needs renewal and improvement. The spiritual decadence of our times demands it. The cultural development of the people demands it. The inner vitality of holy Church demands it. The eternal bidding of Christ, "Do this in memory of Me," demands it.[64]

Renewal must consist in giving life, that is, understanding, participation and beauty, to liturgical worship. This is what the Church proposes to us. We must seek to understand and revitalize the authentic elements that make up liturgical worship; the divine element first, and then the instructive and esthetic elements, with which approved tradition has clothed it.[64]

We cannot be content with having a church full of people, with having a faceless crowd of individuals, a meaningless mass assisting at the sacred rite, distracted in spirit, and without a sense of their inner oneness. We must strive to give a form to those present, an order, an awareness, so as to create the sacred atmosphere in which the religious rite takes place.[64]

The liturgy is the worship of the Mystical Body: those who compose the Mystical Body at a given moment in a given place must be made to feel what they are. They must recognize that they may enter, by means of the priestly rite, into relation with the presence of Christ, and be merged, spiritually, in communion with Him.[64]

The encouragement of the communal sense in the liturgical assembly should not, however, suppress the contribution of personal piety. It should, rather, evoke that contribution and strengthen it. But it should not invade the private spiritual life and the particular sensibility of each one of the faithful, for each remains, at all times, an inviolable person.[64]

Moreover, liturgical education requires other measures. Participation involves first, the use of the senses, seeing and hearing. This fact follows from an awareness that we are part of the economy of the Incarnation, in which the material world becomes epiphany, becomes language.[64]

In other words, the material world is the necessary means for being introduced into the invisible and supernatural world.[64]

Participation demands understanding. It is a fundamental principle that rites should be understood. This does not prevent their having a content rich in mystery, or having portions that only the priests are to recite. But the understanding of the rite is a rule that flows from the rite itself.[64]

The rite is a sign; it is language; rite is the expression of a divine truth communicated to men, and of a human truth addressed to God.[64]

Light is the atmosphere of the liturgy; its voice is wisdom.[64]

The variety of its forms, the dramatic unfolding of its rites, the elevated style of its language, the continual use of sign and symbol, the theological depth of the words and the mysteries fulfilled—all seem to conspire to impede the understanding of the liturgy.[64]

This is true for modern man, especially accustomed as he is to reducing everything to a complete intelligibility and to believing that he understands a truth when he knows how to impart it representationally in a geometrical figure or in a memorable phrase.[64]

We must show the faithful how to understand the Church's prayer, lest we see them turn away from it, feeling themselves excluded from its inner spiritual mys-

teries. The culture of their secular lives has accustomed
them to understanding and knowing all about everything
in their environment and field of interest. We must, therefore, change the difficulty presented by the liturgical rite
into a help for understanding the meaning of Catholic
worship, a meaning that is hidden but impressive, inexhaustible, and living, too.[64]

The mysteries of Christ, brought to life by the liturgy,
should make a profound impression on the life of the
faithful as a congregation and as individual believers. The
grand and dramatic vision of the high mysteries from
which our salvation flows should not be disturbed by the
unrelated insertion of other solemnities or particular de-
votions.[64]

Care must always be taken to preserve in worship the
true proportions of dogma. Souls must be given the sense
of Christ, Who is the focus of our spiritual life, and religion must be a tribute of praise and of love to God,
rather than a set of devotional practices that are arbitrary or utilitarian.[64]

It is in the liturgical-sacrificial and sacramental celebration that the ministry of the Word has its most profound roots and from which it receives its strength and
effectiveness; a ministry that finds its center at the altar,
its highest expression in love, an exacting love, which is
something that consumes, that burns.[43]

In general our contact with the Church is through the
parish, that small, intimate portion of the Church. It is,
like the whole Church, a community of persons, a family,
which witnesses to and foreshadows the heavenly community of the blessed.[59]

The ancient structure of the parish has an indispensable

mission, which is of supreme importance today. To it belongs the responsibility of creating a true community of the Christian people. It is for the parish to initiate and to bring together the people in the normal expression of its liturgical life. It is for it, too, to conserve and to make real the faith in the people of today, to bring to them the saving Gospel of Christ and to practice among them in prayer and humble labor the charity that is goodness and brotherhood.[1]

In the parish everyone has something to give, to do, and not merely to receive.[59]

The liturgy teaches the true meaning of personal integrity, the true direction of a regenerated social sense, the true aim of human activity, of loving and of suffering, the final overcoming of death in the certainty of the resurrection. And it teaches them precisely as fruitful principles to be introduced into the current of the secular world.[64]

The schema on sacred liturgy has been brought to a happy conclusion, and today we may see in this an acknowledgment of a right order of values and duties. God of course comes first, prayer is our first duty, and the liturgy is the first school of spirituality, the first gift we can bestow upon Christians who believe and pray with us. It is the first invitation to the world to break forth in happy and truthful prayer and to feel the life-giving force that comes from joining us in the song of divine praise and of human hope, through Christ our Lord and in the Holy Spirit.[65]

It would be good to treasure this fruit of our Council as something that should animate and characterize the life of the church. For the church is a religious society, a community at prayer. It is composed of people with a flourishing interior life and spirituality that is nourished by faith and grace.[65]

If now we wish to simplify our liturgical rites, if we wish to render them more intelligible to the people and accommodated to the language they speak, we certainly do not intend by this to lessen the importance of prayer, or to give it less prominence than other forms of the sacred ministry or pastoral activity, or to reduce its expressive force and artistic charm.[65]

On the contrary, we desire to make the liturgy more pure, more authentic, more in agreement with the source of truth and grace, more likely to be transformed into a spiritual heritage of the people.[65]

XIII
SACRED ART

I SPEAK from my point of view as a priest, as a churchman who looks upon artists always with a strong hope. We need them. We who are dedicated to religion must make intelligible to man an invisible, supernatural world. Our mysterious treasure cannot be communicated except in the manner of sacrament; that is, by the sacred and sensible sign of art: the sound of words that make music, the color of things that beguile, the forms of wisdom made visible; in other words, by way of the materialization of the spiritual.[66]

We honor the artist who fulfills an almost priestly ministry close to our own. We celebrate the mysteries of God. The artist is a collaborator who seeks to describe these mysteries in immediate and accessible terms.[66]

Yet artists today seem to have renounced the creation of intelligible work, while the critics have their own esoteric language, which demands an initiation if one wishes to arrive at understanding.[66]

We the public, meanwhile, make agitated efforts to grasp some sort of meaning. We had thought of the realm of art as a beatitude; it has become a suffering and a confusion to us.[66]

May I be frank? You have to a degree abandoned us; you have gone to drink at other fountains, seeking, however lawfully, to express things that are not ours.[110]

But in all sincerity I admit that we, too, have caused you pain. We have done this by imposing imitation on you as the first canon of your art, you who are creators constantly giving life to a thousand new ideas and innovations! [110]

Forgive us! We have sometimes weighed you down with a cloak of lead; and then we have abandoned you. We did not speak openly to you nor did we lead you into the secret cell where the mysteries of God make the heart of man leap up with joy, hope, happiness, and rapture.[110]

The language you spoke for our world was docile yet too restrained, too forced, incapable of finding a true freedom of expression. We felt dissatisfied with this expression of yours, and we treated you even more shabbily. We resorted to substitutes, to oleographs, to works of little artistic or real value. We did not have the capacity to understand great and beautiful things, new things, things worthy of being seen. We walked along crooked paths where art and beauty and, what is worse for us, the worship of God were badly served.[110]

One cannot escape the realization that the current artistic idiom is today an irrational and tribalistic abstraction that does not make sense.[66]

The vocation of art is essentially to mediate between the kingdom of the divine mysteries and the world of human souls. Both of these the artist must accept as preestablished realities, not of his own making. Where art has obeyed this vocation, it has raised itself to sublime functions and has rendered incomparable services to the spirit.[64]

We are willing to permit the artist, restless and impatient in the midst of the spiritual clangor of modern life, to engage in the experiment of freedom! You have been told to do as you wish. We no longer ask you to follow either a given tradition, or any one style. Nor will you be obliged to express yourselves in certain proportions or conventional forms.[65]

We ask only that your art serve us in reality and in dignity, that it possess dynamism, that we be able to understand it. We ask further that it may assist us, that it may speak truly and inspire people with authentic religious emotion.[66]

XIV

POPE JOHN XXIII

POPE JOHN PERSONIFIED and expressed so well an essential characteristic of the Catholic Church, namely, universality, that he caused latent energies to leap upward both inside and outside the Church. This happened not only because he shared and favored the progress already made in what is called the internationalization of the Church.[67]

It happened also because, inspired to call together the Ecumenical Council, he took up once more the examination of the great theme of universality, which is the constitutional right of the Church.[67]

In this way, he prepared the spiritual and practical foundation for the harmonious participation of the episcopacy in the responsibility of the government of the entire Church, though not in its actual exercise, which remains personal and unitary. This is to say, he gave to the interior ecumenism of catholicity a canonical development and a spiritual conscience.[67]

This policy rests on two terms, which have been friendly for centuries: the urbis and the orbis, Rome and the world, which, brought closer together, arouse surprising potentialities, announcing a new history for Rome and possibly for the papacy and the world.[67]

To the interior ecumenism of the Church, John XXIII united an exterior ecumenism. His was a double effort, to gather all the separated Christian groups into an organic unity of faith and of charity in the one, holy, Catholic and apostolic Church; also to spread as widely and solidly as possible, peace between the peoples of the earth, between social classes of nations, in short, civil peace to all the earth.[67]

Could we really abandon a way so magistrally traced both for the present as well as for the future by him? There is every reason to think not. And it will be this fidelity to the great principles of his pontificate that will preserve his memory and renown, and that will make us feel him still near to us as a father.[67]

Prophesying is a difficult art. But at this moment, it has become easier and almost a duty, in view of a few postulates put forth by the Pope for whom we grieve. John XXIII pointed out certain paths, which it would be wise for us to know as well as follow. Could we really forget what he incarnated in a certain measure by the human spontaneity of his holy life, namely that the Christian religion is profoundly and essentially capable of giving a new spiritual recharge to the modern world? [67]

Pope John awakened in the conscience of the teaching Church the conviction that Christian doctrine is not merely truth that should be investigated by reason enlightened by faith. It should be also a word productive of life and action.[68]

The authority of the Church, moreover, should not be limited merely to condemning error, but rather should proclaim the positive and living teaching with which it is so fruitfully endowed.[68]

Why did they mourn his death everywhere in the world? What marvel of spiritual convergence produced this thing without precedent in history? [27]

Each one of us experienced an attraction for this man. We know that the sympathy that surrounded him was not an illusion, nor was it the kind of enthusiasm that responds to superficial motives. Rather it was a secret revealing itself, a mystery, which absorbed us.[67]

He inspired in our minds two simple words of great consoling power: truth and charity. He gave us this elementary lesson, rare and difficult to express in reality, which is contained in the words of Saint Paul: "Live according to truth and in charity." [67]

He made us see that truth, religious truth above all, delicate and difficult as it is, inexorably exact in expression, in conception and in profession as it must be, is not made to divide men, nor to kindle in their midst the fire of polemic and dispute. Rather, it should draw them to a unity of thought, be expressed in pastoral care, and infuse souls with the joy of the attainment of brotherhood and of divine life.[67]

This we already knew, but he made us taste the experience; he gave us hope in it and promised us plenitude of life.[67]

Blessed is the Pope who gave to us and to the world the evangelical example of the Good Shepherd.[69]

Blessed is this Pope who showed us that goodness is not weakness or slackness, not an equivocal irenism: that it entails no renunciation of the great rights of truth or duties of authority, but is rather the master virtue of him who represents Christ on earth.[69]

Blessed is the Pope who made us see again that the

authority of the Church is not an ambition to dominate, not an aloofness from the community of the faithful, not a remote and custom-ridden paternalism.[69]

Blessed is this Pope who enabled us to enjoy an hour of fatherhood and spiritual companionship—who taught the world that humanity has need of nothing so much as love.[69]

XV

THE UNITY OF FAITH

IF WE CONSIDER the supreme concept that Christ is our founder, and our head, invisible but real, and that we receive everything from Him so as to constitute together with Him the "total Christ" of Augustine, who permeates the entire theology of the Church, then we shall be better able to understand the chief objectives of the Ecumenical Council.[68]

These are four: the knowledge, or, if you like, the self-awareness of the Church; its reform; the calling together of all Christians in unity; and the dialogue of the Church with the contemporary world.[68]

It is a Council, therefore, of invitation, of hope and of confidence, looking forward to a more widespread, more fraternal participation in its true ecumenicity.[68]

I speak now to the representatives of the Christian denominations separated from the Catholic Church, who have nevertheless been invited to take part as observers in this solemn assembly.[68]

Both my voice and my heart reveal the consolation and hope that their presence gives me, as well as the deep sadness I feel at their prolonged separation.[68]

If any fault for this separation can be laid at our door, we ask pardon for it both from God and from our brothers who may consider themselves to have been offended by us.[68]

This means that the Council is characterized by love, by the most comprehensive and compelling love, by a love that thinks first of others: by the universal love of Christ.[68]

Love fills my soul and the soul of the Church assembled in Council. I look upon our times and their diverse and contrasting manifestations with profound sympathy and with a great desire to give to the men of these times the message of love, of salvation, of hope that Christ brought to the world: "When God sent His Son into the world it was not to reject the world but that the world might find salvation through Him." [68]

This love sustains me now because, as I look at the scene of contemporary human life, I feel somewhat more frightened than comforted, saddened rather than gladdened, summoned almost to speak words that are protective and even condemnatory, rather than to express trust and friendship.[68]

My view of the world fills me with sadness because of its many evils. Atheism has invaded a part of the human race and it brings in its wake an imbalance in the intellectual, moral and social order.[68]

We must be realists, and not conceal the evil that for many reasons and from many sources touches even this universal synod. We are not so blind as not to see the empty places at this Council! Where are our brothers from those nations where the Church is in chains, and what is the state of religion in those countries? [68]

While the knowledge of nature increases its light in the world, darkness continues to fall over the knowledge of God, and thus over the true knowledge of man. While progress continues to perfect every kind of instrument which man uses, his heart is yielding to emptiness, sadness and despair.[68]

Yet may the world know this: the church looks at it with profound understanding; with a sincere intention not to conquer, but to serve it; not to despise it, but to appreciate it; not to condemn it, but to strengthen and save it.[68]

From the window of the Council, opened wide on the world, the Church looks to the peoples of the world with particular solicitude: it looks to the poor, the needy, the afflicted, the hungry, the suffering and the sorrowing.[68]

It looks to men of culture and learning, to scientists, and to artists. For them the Church has great esteem, and it strongly desires to receive from them the fruit of their talent and genius, and in return to strengthen their intellectual life and to defend their liberty.[68]

The Church looks to the workers, to the legitimacy of their hopes, to the need, which they still feel deeply, of social improvement and of an interior uplifting, to the mission that can be theirs, if it is good and if it is Christian, of creating a new world, a world of free men and brothers.[68]

It looks to the leaders of nations, and instead of the grave words of warning that the church must often address to them, it substitutes today a word of encouragement and of confidence: "Take courage, you who rule the nations of the world. Today you can give to your peoples the good things that are necessary for their life: bread, education, work, order, the dignity of free and peaceful citizens. You can do this provided that you know truly who man is, and only Christian wisdom can show you this in its fulness. Working together in justice and love, you can create peace, that greatest of goods, which is so longed for and which the church so strongly defends and promotes, and you can make humanity a single city. May God be with you." [68]

If we seek to define the Ecumenical Council, which apparently had no reason for being except by way of convocation by John XXIII and at a moment when nobody expected it because there were no grave problems to resolve or opinions to conciliate, it will be necessary to seek to understand where the Church wishes to go with this Council. What is its direct scope? To hold out a hand to those who are far from us? Yes, but this is a subordinate question. The Church would not extend the hand to those who are far from us if separation itself could not be defined. [70]

This is the point. The Church is seeking self-knowledge. But you will say to me: "Already for some twenty centuries it has done this." I say to you: "The knowledge that the Church has of itself is progressive." If indeed we are open to the invitation that the Lord makes to us in the Gospel—when, for example, He called on His questioners, His contemporaries, to beware of the signs that approached—it is necessary that we prepare ourselves to see the signs of the times. [70]

The hour has sounded in history when the Church which expresses itself in us and which from us receives structure and life, must say of itself what Christ intended and willed it to be. [117]

There is a maturity in the Church today, there is a presence that enriches it, an experience that it communicates, there is an effort to understand even more, there is a grace of God, which works within the Church and which brings it to a deeper knowledge of itself.[70]

If I were to say to you in the words of ecclesiastical law: "The priest is the minister of worship, etc.," the definition would be exact. But I take Canon Law and I find: "Priests are collaborators of bishops, etc." This is true also. Both statements are true. My point is this: does the rational and juridic expression, which we give to the Church, exhaust the reality that the Church represents; does it say everything? Or is it not silent about much more? [70]

The Church is reflecting on itself. It has need of defining itself. It has a need of knowing itself better, of individuating in some manner the inexpressible realities it carries within itself.[70]

The consciousness of the Church will be defined in the Council even if it remains a kind of open window on the infinite, rather than the confined, the logical and dogmatic perimeter, avoiding the inadequacy of a precise concept. It is the *mysterium ecclesiae*.[70]

I ask again: what is the Ecumenical Council doing? The Church is seeking itself. With a great and moving effort, it is seeking to define itself, to understand what it truly is. The Church, after twenty centuries of presence in history and in the field of human activity, has come to a moment in which it seems to be submersed by the creativity and by the vivacity and by the dimensions of modern history.[71]

The Church has felt the need of recollection. It has felt the need of reassembling itself, of fortifying itself, of purifying itself, of reforming itself and of taking up with great courage and with new energy its path through history.[71]

This self-awareness of the Church is clarified by a faithful commitment to the words and thought of Christ, by a reverent remembrance of the authoritative teaching of ecclesiastical tradition, and by docility to the interior illumination of the Holy Spirit, Who asks of the Church today that it do everything possible to become known as it truly is.[68]

The characteristic of this Council, while aiming expressly at some notable reforms, derives from a desire to call forth the good rather than to escape some present evil. Today the Church, by the grace of God and the merit of so many good and holy Christians, is rather in a state of suffering and of weakness, than in a state of scandal and decadence. The condition and aspect of the Church show it as more wounded than sinning, more needful than unfaithful. The Council, therefore, is a Council of positive reforms, rather than of punitive ones; one of exhortation rather than of anathemas.[72]

In this sense the Council is to be a second spring, a reawakening of the mighty spiritual and moral energies that lie dormant in the Church. The Council evidences a determination to bring about a rejuvenation both of the interior forces of the Church and of the norms by which her canonical structure and liturgical forms are regulated.[68]

In other words, the Council is striving to increase in the Church that beauty of perfection and holiness that imitation of Christ and mystical union with Him in the Holy Spirit alone can confer.[68]

Reform has been through the centuries the renewing ferment of Catholic tradition.[72]

Reform, therefore, is a perennial effort in the Church, which tends to bring the divine idea close to reality, and to put the human reality in touch with the divine.[72]

Yes, the Council aims at renewal. Note well, however, that in saying and desiring this we do not imply that the Catholic Church of today can be accused of substantial infidelity to the mind of its divine Founder. Rather, it is the deeper realization of its substantial faithfulness that fills it with gratitude and humility and inspires it with the courage to correct those imperfections that are a part of human weakness.[68]

The reform at which the Council aims is not, therefore, an overthrowing of the Church's present way of life or a breaking with what is essential and worthy of veneration in its tradition. It is rather an act of homage to that tradition, by stripping it of what is unworthy or defective.[68]

We must guard against thinking that the Council will decree radical and bewildering reforms in the present structure of the Church, changes that will alter its appearance in time and make it a wholly new institution.[72]

The present juridical structure of the Church certainly has need of some renovation, but the Church cannot be substantially changed. It is not the result of infidelity to the genuine mind of Christ. It is rather the result of an historical experience lived always with a rigorous intention of coherence and of fidelity to the spirit of the divine Founder.[72]

No matter what its importance to the Church, no Council is a permanent institution such as a parliament. It is not a synthesis of the whole Church; it does not transform the Church into a corporation represented and directed by a sovereign assembly to which the Pope himself is subject.[72]

The Council is an episode in the life of the Church, a particular moment that calls forth the supreme authority of the Church. But it does not create that authority; it exercises it.[72]

Each of us has some imaginative concept of himself as a reformer of the Church, and naturally each hopes that the time has come for the realization of his dream. If the Council corresponds to the plans of God, it is difficult, no matter how fine our own plans, to see how it will respond to our exact desires.[72]

It is not necessary that the Council correspond to our particular viewpoint; we ought rather enter into the general perspectives of the Council. To believe that the Council will be able to repair human fragility and immediately bring about perfection in the Church and in the world is an ingenuous dream. To hope that it will remedy the many inconvenient practices and also the many theoretical imperfections in Catholic life which each one meets within his own experience as a member or observer is to hope too much.[72]

The final objective of the Council will be to seek to build a bridge to the contemporary world.[68]

How contradictory this seems! While the Church is trying to renew in its interior life the spirit of the Saviour, by distinguishing and detaching itself from profane society in which it is involved, it is at the same time establishing itself as the ferment and instrument of salvation of this very world.[68]

It is discovering and confirming its missionary vocation with ever greater conviction. It is reaffirming that its essential purpose is to make of humanity, in whatever condition it finds it, the object of its mission and passionate zeal.[68]

You, yourselves, my brother bishops, know of what I speak. Indeed, at the beginning of the work of the first session, inspired by the words Pope John XXIII had spoken, you felt the need of addressing to the world a vibrant message of salvation, of fraternity, and of hope.[68]

An unusual but admirable gesture! One could say that the prophetic charism of the Church had suddenly burst forth! And just as Peter on the day of Pentecost felt himself moved to raise his voice immediately and to speak to the people, you likewise wished to give your attention not to those matters of immediate concern to you but to those of the world, and to open the dialogue not only between yourselves but with the world.[68]

Thus the Church intends through the Council to come into contact with the world. This is a great act of charity. The Church will not think only of itself: the Church will think of all humanity. To this end it will seek to be all things to all men: it will seek to be poor, simple, humble and lovable in its language and manner.[72]

The Church will seek to make itself understood. It will give to the men of today the opportunity to hear its voice and to itself the opportunity to speak to men with ease in the language of the times.[72]

The Church wishes to weave a dialogue. This would not be difficult were it not for the radical and profound bewilderment found in the world concerning the notion of God, of Christ, and of the eternal life. The Church seeks to attain almost by itself the prophetic strength of saying to the world, of speaking to modern civilization and to future ages, words that should be corrective and directive.[71]

What then is the Church doing? It seeks not only itself but the world. It seeks to come into new contact with a world that has appropriated to itself the principles of Christianity.[71]

The most beautiful—liberty, humanity, the cult of man, the respect for the human personality, the desire for peace, the desire for unity—are all Christian principles, which the world has made its own. Feeling itself secure in this patrimony, it rebels against Christianity and the Church, against religion, and says: "I will not serve you further, I do not wish any more of you." And we sense that the world, while it rests upon principles that are radically Christian, is opposed to the Church of God.[71]

In this extraordinary contingency the Church rises, it marshals its forces and seeks to come again into contact with the world and to say to it: I know what you are. In great part, at least, whatever you possess that is civilized is a reflection of my principles, of my truth. I can speak to you familiarly because you are in a certain sense my son. It is Christianity that has renewed you and given you your true meaning.[71]

The vision of the Church embraces vast spheres of human life: the new generation, the youth who hope to live fully and to assert themselves; the emerging nations who are becoming conscious of themselves as a people, acquiring their independence and developing their national

structures; the innumerable human beings who feel themselves isolated in the midst of the current of a society
that has no word of truth for their souls.[68]

To all, to all, it extends its proclamation of hope! To
all it offers the light of truth, of life and of salvation, since
"it is God's will that all men should be saved and be led
to recognize the truth." [68]

It should not come as a surprise that, after twenty centuries of Christianity and the great geographical and
historical development of other Christian bodies distinguished by the name of Church, there should still be a
need for a more precise definition of the true, profound
and complete nature of the Church that Christ founded
and that the apostles began to build.[68]

The Church is a mystery. It is a reality imbued with
the divine presence and, for that reason, it is ever capable
of new and deeper investigation.[68]

To the living Christ the living Church responds. If
faith and charity are the principles of its life, it is clear
that nothing should be neglected to give our faith a joyful
certitude and a renewed nourishment.[68]

May this Council be fully aware of this multiple but
simple, fixed yet moving, mysterious yet clear, relationship between ourselves and the blessed Christ. Between
this holy and living Church of which we are a part, and
Christ, from Whom we come, by Whom we live, and to
Whom we are going. May no other light shine, save Christ,
may no other truth concern us save the words of the
Maker. May no other aspiration guide us other than to
be absolutely faithful to Him.[68]

Let us rejoice, my brothers, for when was the Church
ever so aware of itself, so in love with Christ, so blessed,

so united, so willing to imitate Him, so ready to fulfill His mission? [65]

Let us rejoice, because we have learned to understand one another and to deal with one another, and though we had almost become strangers, through the process of union we have become friends. [65]

Our satisfaction is in no way diminished by the variety, by the multiplicity, or even by the divergence of the opinions that have been expressed in the discussions of the Council. On the contrary, this is a proof of the depth of the subjects investigated, of the interest with which they have been followed, and, of the freedom with which they have been discussed. [65]

It has, moreover, stirred up in all of us that charity which must always be present in our search for and profession of the truth. The pastoral purpose of the Council has been brought into focus through the discussions, which have always tried to find means and expressions capable of closing the gap between our separated brethren and ourselves. Thus its every act has been accompanied by God, the source of all hope. [65]

Yet, even so, it leaves us with an even more vivid realization of what remains to be done and with a more deeply felt sense of our duty of making the Church better fitted to deliver its message of truth and salvation to the modern world. We have not forgotten the conditions of our times, nor has our love for the men among whom we live grown less. As each one returns home to his ordinary affairs, he will carry in his heart an earnest concern to make that charity more effective. [65]

The Church has wished to grow in its consciousness and understanding of itself. It has begun a profound meditation on that mystery from which it draws its origin and form. The meditation is not finished. The very difficulty of concluding it reminds us of the depth and breadth of this doctrine, and challenges us to try to understand and to express the doctrine in a way that cannot fail to lead our minds and those of the faithful to Christ Himself, from Whom all gifts come to us and to Whom we wish to return all we have. Our efforts cannot fail to increase both our happiness in being personally called to form part of this holy mystical body of Christ, as also our mutual charity, the principle and law of the life of the Church.[65]

If, once the Council is finished, there were to be a persecution, it would not be remarkable. Why? Because we are becoming importune as were the apostles, as was the Christian in Roman society when he denied the divinity of the emperor. Since the Christian message expressed fulness and evidence the world sought to suffocate it.[70]

I would say humanly speaking that in the light of history there would be nothing illogical if, because the Church is speaking again with such a voice, a type of modern mentality would seek to combat it and to destroy it. Instead, what the Pope awaits, what the Church awaits, is the possibility of a new colloquy, the possibility of a new announcement, of new friendships, of new hopes, of new compassion for the world which surrounds us.[70]

God loved the world, Christ came into this world that crucified Him, into this world made for us poor mortals, full as we are of misery, infidelity and mediocrity. Jesus came to love us. What a stupendous work! This is why I speak of mission. This is why I say to Christians that they should become apostles, why I speak of social communication, of making contact, this is why I speak of unity in the Church, of the intellectual message. This is why I speak of those who are far from us in order that the radiation of love that is lighted in the heart and very soul of the Church and that scatters, explodes and diffuses itself may be communicated to all the world as a message of hope, of goodness, of light, of life and of evangelical salvation.[70]

I am so convinced that for the final, happy conclusion of this Council prayers and good works are necessary that, after careful deliberation and much prayer, I have decided to become a pilgrim myself to the land of Jesus, our Lord.[65]

In fact, if God is with me, I intend to go to Palestine to honor personally, in the holy places where Christ was born, lived, died and ascended to heaven, the first mysteries of our faith, the Incarnation and the Redemption.[65]

I shall see that blessed land from which Peter came and to which not one of his successors has returned. I shall return there as an expression of prayer, penance and renewal to offer Christ His Church, to call our separated brothers to this one holy Church, to beg divine mercy on behalf of peace among men, that peace that shows in these days how weak and feeble it is, and to beseech Christ our Lord for the salvation of the entire human race.[65]

XVI

THE HOLY LAND:
A PILGRIM OF PEACE

MY JOURNEY is that of Peter's witness. I, together with the whole Church, stand with Peter at Caesarea Philippi, and say to Jesus: Yes, Lord, You are the Christ, the Son of the living God.[25]

It is a pilgrimage of offering. As the Magi from the East, the precursors and prototypes of all peoples of the earth, so I from the West wish to bring to Jesus the offering of His Church, and to acknowledge in Him its Founder and Master, its Lord and Saviour.[25]

It is a journey of questing and of hope. I seek all those who are sons and brothers to us in Christ, in the setting of the Gospels, conjured up by that land of benediction. How can I avoid asking myself: Where is the full flock of Christ? Where are the lambs and the sheep of His fold? Are they all here? Which ones are missing? And so I can only implore Jesus the Good Shepherd, using His own words: "May there be one fold and one shepherd." [25]

And my heart reaches out also to those outside the fold of Christ. My good wishes embrace all the peoples of the earth, with feelings of respect and of love, wishing them happiness and peace.[25]

It is thus a pilgrimage of prayer, made in humility and love. The whole world is present to my heart. No one is forgotten.[25]

I wish my very first words to express the emotions I feel at seeing with my own eyes and treading with my own feet that land where the patriarchs, our fathers in the faith, once lived; this land that through the centuries has resounded with the voices of the Prophets speaking in the name of the God of Abraham, Isaac and Jacob. This land, finally and especially, which the presence of Jesus Christ blessed and hallowed forever for all Christians and, one might say, for the entire human race.[73]

From this land, unique in all the world for the greatness of the events of which it has been the theater, my humble prayer is raised to God for all men, believing and unbelieving, and I happily include the sons of the "People of the Covenant" whose part in the religious history of mankind can never be forgotten.[73]

A pilgrim of peace, I pray before all else for the favor of man's reconciliation with God and for a true peace among all men and all peoples. May God hear my prayer since He is a God, as the prophet proclaims, Who thinks "thoughts of peace and not of affliction." May He bestow upon today's tormented world the incomparable gift, which echoes throughout the pages of the Bible, and in which I am happy to summarize my greeting, my prayers and my wishes: Shalom, Shalom—Peace, Peace.[73]

I wished my journey to Palestine to take on the meaning of a particular, fervent, loving meeting with Christ. I desired it to be a proclamation to all the world of the exalted reality and universality of the Redemption that the Divine Saviour continues to effect through His Church.[75]

I bear forever in my heart the memories of that humble visit to the holy places, and of the warm welcome given to me by the people of that sacred land. May God reward them, may He wipe away their tears, and grant them peace, prosperity and true happiness.[74]

And, after that journey, setting foot again on the soil of Italy, where Peter landed, I can say that I have kept faith with my pledge.[75]

You understand that my journey was more than a singular and spiritual incident. It has become an event, which can have great historic importance and be a link that binds us to a secular tradition. It is probably the beginning of new events, which may be of benefit to the Church and to humanity.[75]

One might almost think that Peter had just left this place; what capped my surprise was that the welcome extended to Peter came not only from my own brothers in the faith, but also from my brothers separated from me for centuries. It came, as well, from Moslems and Jews, who amiably sought to acclaim this unexpected, yet natural, return.[76]

I felt myself the object of such a general and enthusiastic welcome at each stage of my journey that I feel obliged to attribute it to causes beyond the human.[77]

My journey was as the passing of a plow over earth grown hard and unyielding. It challenged the conscience of all with thoughts and divine designs buried but not defaced by centuries of history, and which now seem to waken to prophetic hope.[76]

Never has the past that enshrined the Scriptures appeared so real to the memory, and never has it reflected simple facts; simple, yes, but splendid and rich in promise too, straining toward an unknown future which I perceive as full of great and good things.[76]

I wish that pondering on the meaning of all this would continue, and not only in me, who feel it a duty and a need, but in all the faithful; in those who understand, think, and know how to decipher the "signs of the times," as Jesus has said.[76]

The return to the Gospels should be our continual action in thought, spiritual fervor, moral renewal, and religious and human sensibility. This return does not demand an actual voyage to these places sanctified by the life of our Lord. Yet it requires an always loving and attentive knowledge of its epiphany, of its manifestation to the world.[76]

The responsibility that the Lord has given me as a successor of the Apostles fills me with a conscious desire for the union of Christians and all that can contribute towards re-establishing perfect understanding among them.[77]

Let us entrust the past to the mercy of God and listen to the advice of the Apostle: "Forgetting those things which are behind, and reaching forth unto those things which are before, I press toward the mark for the prize of the high calling of God in Christ Jesus . . . because Jesus Christ has made me His own." He has made us His own through the same baptism, the same priesthood, the offering of the same Eucharist, the one sacrifice of the one Lord of the Church.[77]

No one can forget that when God, as Man, wished to choose a fatherland, a tongue, a family in this world, he chose the East.[78]

Every nation received the good seed of the preaching

of the Gospel with the mentality and culture proper to it. Each local church developed with its own personality, practices, and usages intact. It celebrated in its own way the mysteries of the faith without in any way doing harm to the unity of the faith and the union of all in charity, and respect for the order established by Christ.[78]

This is the origin of our diversity in unity, of our catholicity, an essential mark of the Church of Christ of which the Holy Spirit in our time, especially in the Council, is giving us a new experience.[78]

Even as unity is not catholic if it does not protect the legitimate differences between people, so diversity is not catholic except in the measure that it respects unity, serves charity, and contributes to the growth "of the holy people of God." [78]

If the meaning of "Catholic" truly penetrates us, all egoism is conquered, all class-consciousness yields to social solidarity, all nationalism gives way to the good of the world community, all racism is condemned, totalitarianism revealed in its inhumanity. The small heart cracks, or better, it achieves a tremendous capacity to expand.[112]

And this unity that is ours we show forth above all within the family of the Church, with a collaboration without strife and with only one concern, the good of the faithful. Let us show too, as far as possible, that unity that, although incomplete and wounded, already exists with our other Christian brothers. I have said on another occasion: "Do they not have the same baptism, the same fundamental faith, the same priesthood, which offers the one sacrifice of the one Lord of the Church?" [78]

We should not forget that our neighbor, him whom we should love as ourselves, is not alone our Christian brother.[78]

We have a splendid array of Eastern rites, which have always been in perfect communion with Rome. I send my greeting to all these Churches and along with the greeting, I say to these communities: May glory, honor, consolation, comfort and grace be yours! God bless you for bearing your many burdens, for your loyalty when persecuted, your exact and firm adherence to your traditions, your defense of the teaching handed down to you by the Fathers. May God bless you especially for your invincible loyalty.[79]

All Catholics know how the Church of Rome, today more than ever, opens her heart and extends her arms to the Catholic communities of the Eastern rites.[79]

The Church regards as incomparable wealth the variety of languages and rites in which it maintains its dialogue with heaven. The eastern communities who continue in their noble and ancient traditions are, in our eyes, worthy of honor, esteem and confidence.[79]

In all love I exhort the venerable Eastern Churches to have confidence in the Apostolic See, and above all to have the courage to persevere in that which has given them their double title to glory: a wholehearted fidelity to their origins and an unfailing loyalty to the successor of Peter.[80]

The very existence in the Church of different rites and languages leads us to consider those other Churches deriving from the one stem, which is Christ our Lord, but that are not in full communion with the Church of Rome. They have the same baptism, the same fundamental faith, a valid hierarchy and sacraments that are effective channels of grace.[79]

I send my respectful greetings to these ancient and great Eastern Churches. Let me convey my respects with the sincerity and with the fraternal and simple gesture of the spirit that moved us to authorize the visit to Moscow of a bishop of the Catholic Church.[79]

The object was to pay homage, to show that there is no reason for rivalry or prestige, for pride or ambition, no desire to prolong discords or differences, which in the past perhaps may have seemed justified, but which today appear wholly outdated.[79]

I also venture to make my own the spontaneously generous call of my predecessors, especially of John XXIII. I wish that I might have the trumpet voice of an angel saying: Come! Let the barriers that separate us fall, let us discuss the questions of doctrine that divide us and that are still the object of controversy.[79]

Let us seek to make our creed a common one, give it articulation, and join together our hierarchical union! I want neither to absorb nor to suppress the whole of this great flowering of Eastern Churches, but I would like to see them regrafted upon the one tree of Christian unity.[79]

Such a cry becomes a prayer. I pray that though it may be too much to ask for in our age, coming ages at least might see restored the unity of those who are still true Christians, especially the unity with these venerable and holy Eastern Churches.[79]

What is lacking that this may come about? Is it perhaps that we Catholics are without sufficient understanding of the great religious traditions of the Eastern Churches?

Are they, for their part, aware of our feelings, of the legitimate sense in which our traditions have developed and of the truths which must be acknowledged by those who believe in Christ? [79]

I cannot tell. I only know that the Gospel contains a remarkable word, one of the rare words that the evangelists have preserved in the original way it was used by Christ. This word is *"Ephphetha,"* which means, "Open up!" The Lord gave power of hearing and power of speech to one who was deaf and dumb and who, in the interpretation of some scholars, represents mankind.[79]

We are all a little deaf, we are all a little dumb. May the Lord open our ears and loosen our tongues! May the Lord enable us to hear the voices of history, the voices of the spirit, His own voice, the echoing Gospel, still our law and power because it is the word of God.[79]

May He give us strength and grace to hear the word of God and the ability to say unanimously, with one voice: Holy, Holy, Holy: Honor and glory to the Eternal Father, the Divine Son, the Holy Spirit. When that happens we shall have anticipated our paradise on earth, making in the history of man, and above all in that of the Church, a great springtime of new life, of hope, of salvation, and of peace in the world.[79]

My emotion is deep and my joy profound in this truly historic hour. After centuries of silence and of waiting, the Catholic Church and the Patriarchate of Constantinople meet once again in the person of their highest representatives.[80]

An ancient Christian tradition lovingly sees as the center of the world that place upon which the glorious Cross of the Saviour was erected and where He, "being raised up from the earth, draws all things unto Himself." [80]

It was fitting then and providential that it should be in this place, this forever blessed and sacred place, that we, pilgrims from Rome and Constantinople, should be able to meet and be united in a common prayer.[80]

You [the Patriarch Athenagoras] have desired this meeting ever since the time of my unforgettable predecessor John XXIII, for whom you did not conceal your esteem and affection, and to whom, with striking insight, you applied the words of the evangelist: "There was a man sent from God, whose name was John." [80]

Doubtless, on the one side and on the other side, the roads that lead to union may be long and strewn with difficulties. But these two paths converge and reach the sources of the Gospel. Is it not, then, a happy augury that today's meeting takes place in that land where Christ founded His Church and shed His blood for it? [80]

It is in any case an eloquent manifestation of the great good will that increasingly inspires Christians who are worthy of that name. It is the will to work to overcome disunity, to break down barriers in the will to work resolutely on the road that leads to reconciliation.[80]

Differences of a doctrinal, liturgical and disciplinary nature will have to be examined, at the proper time and place, in a spirit of fidelity to truth and of understanding in charity.[80]

What can and must now begin to develop is that fraternal charity, which is resourceful in finding new ways to express itself, and which, learning from the past, is ready to pardon, more ready to believe good than evil, careful above all to conform itself to the Divine Master and to allow itself to be drawn and transformed by Him.[80]

May the Risen Christ, by whose death we are reconciled to the Father, be our inspiration in our efforts to restore the unity of all those who are redeemed by Him and who believe in His name.[108]

I look with reverence on the religious patrimony conserved and developed among our separated brothers. I am pleased with the study made by those of the Roman Church who wish to witness and to honor the authentic treasures of truth and of the spiritual life possessed by them in the hope of improving our relationship with them.[65]

I hope also that it will be with a similar desire that they, in turn, will wish to study more deeply the logical and linear descent of our doctrine from divine revelation, our history and our religious life.[65]

Let us not cease to hold quiet and reverent meetings with our separated brothers, who will not refuse calm and friendly discussions. Being more solicitous for their convenience than for our honor, let us seek by what ways and means brotherly union may be restored.[109]

To approach one another, to meet one another, to greet one another, to get to know one another, to talk to one another: what could be simpler, more natural, more human? Certainly this is true. But there is even more in all of this: listening to one another, praying for one another; and, after so many years of separation, after so many painful controversies, loving one another.[83]

Be assured of my respect, esteem and desire to establish the best possible relations with you in our Lord. My attitude conceals no hidden snares, no intention of concealing the difficulties that lie in the way of a complete and final understanding. It does not fear the intricacies of discussion nor the anguish of waiting. Good faith and charity are the foundation stones I offer you.[82]

The esteem which I have for you personally and for the institutions and Christian values you represent makes it possible for me to join with you in facing the great dialogue whose length, given the still unsolved doctrinal differences, no one can determine. But trust that the Lord Jesus Christ, to whom we are all linked by faith and baptism, fills our heart with a gentle, powerful hope.[82]

And that is not all. The question must be asked: In which direction does one instinctively turn when one wishes to understand the encounter (at the highest level, that of responsibility) between the Catholic Church and the other Christian confessions? We are tempted to look backwards to the past. But this would mean getting lost in the labyrinth of history and would certainly reopen wounds that are not yet completely healed.[82]

I took the liberty of talking, above all, of Christian forgiveness: reciprocal if possible. "Let us all give and seek forgiveness" (Horace). We have need of this peace if we are to enter into friendly relations and easy dialogue.[82]

The dialogue is not proud, it is not bitter, it is not offensive. Its authority is intrinsic to the truth it explains, to the charity it communicates, to the example it proposes; it is not a command, it is not an imposition. It is peaceful, it avoids violent method, it is patient, it is generous.[115]

It is best not to look to the past, but to the present,

and above all to the future. Others may and must study the past; I prefer to turn my attention now to what should be, not to what has been.[82]

I am looking toward the truth of something new, a dream which must become reality. Let me quote the words of St. Paul: "Forgetting what I have left behind, intent on what lies before me, I press on with the goal in view, eager for the prize, God's heavenly summons in Christ Jesus." [82]

Hope is our guide, prayer our power, and charity our method, in the service of divine truth which is our faith and our salvation.[82]

These developments, for which you pray, for a "concrete and historical" theology "centered on the history of salvation," I willingly support, and the suggestion seems worthy of being further studied.[82]

May I once more draw your attention to the words: "We have set out together on a road." That is to say: we have not yet reached our destination.[82]

I am not hoping for miraculous or immediate solutions. The fruit for which I hope must ripen slowly, through study and prayer. And reconciliations that are merely superficial or apparent or improvised, concealing difficulties instead of solving them, will, far from helping, delay our progress.[82]

As for us, like the Watchman of whom Isaiah speaks: "Watchman, how long the night?" We are on the alert, seeking to see, happy each time we do, these signs in the heart of night heralding the dawn. These are signs that some progress has been made in the dialogue which has begun, some step forward toward a reconciliation with

those who are sustained by the same Gospel and whose
hearts resound the same joyful cry of St. Paul to the
Ephesians: "One Lord, one faith, one baptism, one God
and Father of all, Who is above all and through all, and
in you all." [82]

XVII

THE HUMAN MISSION
OF THE CHRISTIAN

TODAY, more than ever before, the Catholic laity throughout the world is called upon to make the mission of the Church its own, not only as collaborators but personally and spontaneously.[60]

The spiritual vitality our laity possesses is not yet properly understood or preached. The laity itself must first understand it. This vitality is not given to them that their reach may exceed the priest's grasp. It is given to them simply because the layman is a Christian.[4]

Within his conscience a voice speaks: If I am a Christian I should acknowledge my good fortune and proclaim my vocation. If I am a Christian I should not be a negative, passive, even hostile element in the outpouring of the spirit that Christianity communicates to souls. I, too, must be involved and immersed in this flow of grace. I must become no less than one who is sound, who assists, and who echoes the call of the Church.[4]

It should never be forgotten that in the area of temporal concerns, religious and moral principles apply, and a Christian can never be detached in his activity, no matter how centered in the profane it may be, from the law of God. In every activity he must have an apostolic spirit, which, by reason of his virtuous life, makes the Christian faith shine forth.[60]

Insistence on separate spheres of activity for the Church and the world can be stressed to such a degree as to make the Church a closed cenacle remote from the society in which it finds itself; paralyzed in its doctrinal, pedagogic, charitable and social contribution. It can make the secular world insensitive to religious problems, the greatest in life, and therefore exposed to the recurrent danger of believing itself to be self-sufficient, with all the tragic consequences which this illusion finally entails.[83]

The Catholic in the world cannot neglect the recollection and pledge of his Christian conscience in order to be free to devote himself wholly to the demands of his secular profession.[83]

Unity of psychology, of mentality, of conscience, and of conduct is often obtained today by the unhappy method of simplifying the complex reality of life. But simplification does not occur, because to suppress does not mean to solve. Problems remain, and become the torment of consciences and the disquietude of social life.[83]

The problem of the layman must eventually be resolved within a higher unity, in a genial and harmonious synthesis. Now, however, it presents itself with increasing sensitivity and at times an inner discomfort, because everyone understands that the solution cannot be found in suppressing either of the two elements in question at the moment of conflict.[83]

The faithful layman, in other words, cannot afford to forget that he is a man of this world in order to remain completely a participating member of the Mystical Body.[83]

Christians must not close themselves off in compartments, isolated from the cultural and social setting in which their lives are lived. They must be open and receptive.[83]

We should be conscious of our twofold citizenship in the Church and the world. While the Catholic layman is not ordinarily conscious of it, turning easily to one or the other, it should be remembered how important a thing it is to belong simultaneously to two such distinct societies.[83]

This two-directional orientation possesses the secret of legitimate freedom of conscience and of action, together with the possibility of endowing the autonomous temporal scene with a dignity and a wealth of moral energies that it could not achieve by itself.[83]

It is thus the layman's function, after acknowledging the two citizenships, the ecclesiastical and the temporal, to bring into the professional field his Christian witness, and to bring into the field of Catholic life his secular testimony.[83]

Therefore the first program of the apostolate, of the laity especially, is to present to the world a Christianity that is worthy of admiration, attractive and sympathetic.[60]

Our teaching recognizes participation of the faithful layman in the spiritual priesthood of Christ and therefore his ability and also his responsibility to share in the Church's apostolate. His apostolate expresses different ideas and forms suited to the possibilities and nature of his life. It is an apostolate which imposes itself as a mission proper to our time.[83]

This role entrusted to the laity is not a properly qualified ministry, but an activity shaped in diverse ways, directed at establishing contacts between the religious and the secular life.[83]

The Catholic laity is vested with a function which has become extraordinarily important, and in a sense indispensable; it acts as a bridge between the Church and society. And this is not to insure a means of interference on the part of the Church, a control in the field of temporal matters and in the affairs of this world, but to assure that our world is not left without the message of Christian salvation.[83]

In reference to some activities, the layman's function as bridge becomes a true, proper collaboration in practical needs of great importance: in the scholastic, administrative, legal, social, journalistic, artistic, and charitable fields.[83]

It may be said that from every sector of the layman's secular professions there can be pointed out to the teaching authority and to the ministry of the Church new, interesting and vast problems, which must not be treated empirically, in terms of old handbooks, but which need to be considered in the light of a systematic and scientific research that only the Catholic laity can usefully provide.[83]

We often use the phrase "the consecration of the world," and within the meaning of this phrase special prerogatives in the secular sphere are attributed to the layman for the spreading of the light and grace of Christ. This is possible precisely because he can act upon the secular world from within, as a direct participant in its substance and experience. The priest, on the other hand, who is to a large extent separated from secular life, cannot, generally, exert influence over it except in an extrinsic way, through his words and ministry.[83]

One of the marvels of our times is this: While in former times the hierarchy assumed completely both the responsibility and the exercise of every evangelizing and sanctifying activity in the Church, while the layman remained a docile member of the faithful—a good listener —today the layman has awakened to his vocation. He repeats delightedly: "I too, have a work to do. I cannot remain a passive and insensible member of the Church." [4]

A second marvel: the hierarchy calls the layman today to cooperate with it. It is no longer exclusive, it is not jealous but its summons is stunning in its import. In effect, it says: "Come join us and let us collaborate. Let us work out a harmony of ideas and programs so that we may properly distribute the work that is to be done." [4]

It is the hierarchy itself that asks for the help of the laity. It calls every one and to every one it speaks this reminder. The hour has struck—and it is the hour of the laity! [4]

The attempt to place the work of human and social redemption ahead of the moral and religious has resulted in effects as significant as they have been unfortunate. This has come about not for any reason of practical methodology that certainly can validly suggest beginning the missionary and pastoral work of the Church with the gifts of its human charity, but rather for reasons that are a part of present day thought. Such is the preference for temporal needs over spiritual ones, economic redemption before religious redemption, social reform before moral reform.[60]

The Church seeks above all to communicate the faith, even if for this end it uses its means of charity. Others urge that it is a secondary matter to preach a definitive and obligatory faith, and that it is more suitable to preach some moral precepts, and to spread works of philanthropy and culture.[60]

Apostolic love involves a confrontation with the world which can be full of danger. How far can apostolic relativism go? To what point should intransigence be exercised? How far can a Catholic go in the exercise of tolerance? Those who guide the Church will say: meanwhile the question remains a highly delicate one.[60]

The work of so many men and women in spreading moral and religious ideas that abstract from any homage to Catholic orthodoxy often seems to enjoy a greater efficacy and persuasion precisely because it does not begin at a fixed point, is not bound to determined dogmas, nor burdened by the serious and sublime charge of divine truths.[60]

It is born from a fusion of the genius and fire of these individuals who are so often generous and sincere.[60]

Enriched by some precious fragment of natural morality or by some biblical or philosophical remnant, by some poetic or artistic effusion, or by some generic Christian principle, they begin to preach the conversion of the world. They are apostles in their own names. They preach no truths other than those measured by their own human capacity. They lack any "mystery" that should move and impregnate a true mission of salvation.[60]

Theirs is no longer a religious mission. It is a human mission. It is no longer a continuation of Christ, it is a purely human event.[60]

Orthodoxy is the seal of union, the channel of communication, the guarantee of union with Christ, of His presence and of His authority. It is the indispensable condition for the reception of the divine patrimony and the guarantee of its being preserved intact. From the notion of orthodoxy we understand that the mission of the Church is properly one of communicating transcendent values. It demands therefore that whoever shares in this ministry should be first an apostle before being a teacher; a minister of the word before being its defender; a channel, not a source.[60]

Our modern individualism does not sympathize with a form of thought and of life fixed forever by way of authority. Religious fervor seems to diminish when it must model itself on unchangeable dogma, and fervor is extinguished when it cannot spontaneously follow the impulses of sentiment or employ its own personal experiences.[60]

The man who wishes to be an apostle should be subject to ecclesiastical authority, and not separate himself from it. He should unite, not detach himself. He should offer his services, not insist on his own liberty. He should feel solidarity with the message of the Church and also with its concrete and visible manifestation.[60]

The apostolate is not freely exercised, but is a disciplined commitment, a collaboration. The more it is imbued with the hierarchical and community spirit the more perfect it will be.[60]

There is a tendency among some in the Church to discover and denounce, often with perspicacity but also with bitter irony, all possible defects in those who are close to them in the faith, their fellow Catholics. If their devotion is questionable and their zeal imperfect, they receive censure and mockery. Yet those outside the Church are at the same time receiving from these critics a generous understanding of their many virtues and praiseworthy qualities. For the faithful, there is only reprimand. For those who do not share our faith there is eager recognition of their merit and their virtues.[81]

This expression of moral judgment, which discovers evil in the so-called good, and good in the so-called evil, is, it is true, evocative of the Gospel, which places the pharisee behind the publicans and prostitutes. Further, it contains a Christian criterion, which can have the effect of renovating virtue, by giving to virtue a sincerity, interiorness and humility, and by forbidding that it be expressed in conventional forms which are empty of profound human content and of divine grace.[81]

But the Gospel form of this criterion is also an encouragement not to lose faith and trust in any human being, who is always capable of interior regeneration and needful of a greater mercy. This Gospel judgment supposes a divine authority. And where it is used to effect a purposeful moral analysis, it cannot become stylized, it cannot allow offense to the family of the faithful in order to extol those who are outside it. It ends up by falsifying the very moral judgment it sought to reestablish, by condemning with reckless supposition the faithful in order to gloss over the faults of those who are censurable for failure both in their thinking and in their lives.[81]

And besides, are these Catholics who are so censured indeed pharisees, and do those who are so indulged have the sentiments of repentance of the sinners whom the Gospel rehabilitates? This attitude [of which I speak] is not rare. It has found a large place in contemporary literature (Dostoevski, Mauriac) and has established the reputations of many eminent and venerable preachers. Its supporters too have sometimes seemed disposed to alienate the faithful in order to draw closer to those not of the faith.[81]

The moral austerity of such critics merits attention. But I doubt the effectiveness of their method when it becomes stylized, lacking humility and charity, and when it spreads a spirit of uneasiness rather than one of unity, presenting Christianity under a bitter and one-sided aspect.[81]

Whoever demonstrates intolerance of his place in his father's house loses the capacity to call those outside to enter in, and he exposes himself to the danger that it will be he, the impatient one, who will be tempted to leave the house of the father.[81]

But we must love those whom we wish to evangelize. This is the great design of the apostolate. It is not a selfish interest that moves one to act, but rather the good of others.[61]

The apostolate is not a conquest, it is a service. It is not a condemnation; it is a redemption.[61]

The Church at this moment looks with solicitude on the Catholic laity on all levels, with its varied life and problems. To the Catholic laity, I say: The Church calls you, awaits you, invites you to share its life, to share its genuine values. Yet it does not wish to make you strangers to the currents of modern life, but rather to encourage and strengthen you on your way so that you will not be tossed about in these same currents. Its hope is that you will be the ones to shape these currents and give them meaning, that you may understand and enjoy them as children of God.[43]

There are many Catholics who live in the Church without even thinking that they belong to this Church, to the Mystical Body of Christ, who never think of their duty of feeling every pain, every joy of the Church. Saint Paul says: "We too, all of us, have been baptized into a single body by the power of a single Spirit . . . and if one part is suffering, all the rest suffer with it; if one part is treated with honor, all the rest find pleasure in it." [51]

No one must be a stranger to the life of the Church; all Christians can and must be aware of its great problems. Each one must know that the Lord has called him to his place in the Church. Each must answer his vocation, each must feel himself in communion with the large, universal family of Christ. Our Catholic involvement must enlarge the horizons around us; we must see the world as the field of God, where we also must work.[51]

Thus the hour has struck for those who understand that to be a Christian is a blessing because it involves them precisely in the ministry of salvation. It can, too, be a great burden, and risk, and duty. It means, in effect, to carry, together with the clergy, the Cross of Christ into the very heart of society. It means to preach Christ, around whom always swirls the drama of contradiction—and to carry this drama into our modern world.[4]

XVIII
PASTORAL LOVE

ADOLESCENCE IS THE AGE when "some are called." [8]

This is one of the most interesting and most mysterious phenomena of human psychology—the time of "vocation," the moment of spiritual fulfillment. For some it has meaning merely in a moral sense, but for others it involves religion as well. [8]

The time of vocation comes about when the religious sense manifests itself so compellingly—whether as a spiritual torment or as some kind of attraction or as a sense of joy is not important—that it gives rise to an exalted inward contest between the person's freedom and his sense of duty, a contest that is morally crucial for the rest of his life. [8]

Adolescence is also the time of strenuous intellectual searching, a time when love bursts forth, the period when people are most able to perceive religious values in life and to give to their inherited religion a deep and personal significance. [8]

When this happens, it may find expression in a dramatic moral decision or in the form of some absolute and self-sacrificing loyalty full of passionate though unstable enthusiasm, a splendid burst of generosity, a wonderful surge of aspiration soaring upwards to the heights of heroism and poetry.[8]

Vocation to the priesthood, from its birth to its full development, though principally a gift of God, nevertheless demands the generous cooperation of many persons, both of the clergy and the laity. If in fact modern civilization has nourished among Christians the esteem and search for material goods, it has also snuffed out in many hearts the esteem of supernatural and eternal goods.[84]

Vocation, today, means renunciation, unpopularity, sacrifice, a preference for the interior life, a preference for austere and constant perfecting over unthinking and easy mediocrity. It means the ability to hear the pleading voices of the world, the voices of innocent, suffering souls who know no peace, who are without a guide, without comfort, without love.[84]

At the same time, vocation means the quieting of the disturbing voices of indulgence and egotism. It means understanding the difficult but magnificent mission of the Church. Today, more than ever, it strives to teach man who he is, what is his end and his destiny; and to reveal to faithful souls the immense and ineffable riches of Christ's love.[84]

"Follow me and I will make you fishers of men." These words mean that the work of Redemption is not accomplished on earth and in time without the ministry of consecrated men, of men who, by an offering of themselves, realize the plan of salvation initiated by the divine charity of God.[84]

If God had chosen, His love could have spread of itself and redeemed men directly. But God willed to save men in Christ through the service of men. God not only gave the world a revelation, a religion, He gave it a Church, an organic society, a community equipped with a structure where certain brothers work for the salvation of other brothers. He created a hierarchy; He instituted a priesthood.[84]

Where the message and virtue of the salvation of Christ must reach, there also must the priesthood of Christ extend.[84]

The world as a whole is today more aware of the immense moral and spiritual resources that the Church possesses. The world understands, too, what a decisive and beneficial gift the Church offers to all men of good will who wish to work for the peaceful organization of the life of men on earth. And is there not in all this, using the expression of my predecessor, one of the "signs of the times" that witnesses to and voices man's most cherished hopes? [1]

The bringing of the Gospel to the world, even to the modern world, so secular and so often hostile to religion, depends principally, as Christ wished and as the Church has continually proclaimed, on the clergy. Perhaps no other age in all of history has ever been so estranged and contrary to the priesthood and to its religious mission as is the present. And yet, at the same time, no age has shown itself so needful and open to the pastoral assistance of good and zealous priests.[1]

The Church sends you out, weak among the strong, unarmed among the armed, heralds of love in a world shot through with hatred, prophets of the spirit in the marketplace of the profane, heirs of a tradition and proclaimers of a future in a world without a yesterday and without a tomorrow, wholly committed to the gaining of success today.[85]

The modern world looks at the priest with hostility, blinded in its perspective of him. The heir of the long-dead Middle Ages, the ally of selfish conservatism, the high priest of a silenced litany, the stranger in life: this is the priest. The clergy has felt this aversion of society in the midst of the new needs of the century.[86]

The Church does not guarantee you tranquillity or immunity, but it says to you in the words of Christ: "Do not fear." Today it has need of greater fidelity because of the greater peril of the struggle against it. It has need of greater love because so many of its children no longer turn to it in love. *Nolite timere.* The life you have chosen is grand and perilous. It is not meant for the lowly minded, for the opportunist; it is made for love and for sacrifice.[85]

The heart of a priest should be even more capable of loving than is the heart of a simple member of the faithful.[87]

It is not true to say that love has as its only object what is readily accessible to our immediate experience. It tends by its very nature to transcend the immediate and to seek for motives for loving that are higher than that which is loved.[87]

Human beings are images of God, and to know them in their needs and in their miseries, in their development, and in their changes and all of their vicissitudes, is to be capable of penetrating into their very souls.[87]

You should be capable not only of knowing but of seeking—of seeking those gone astray. My sons, if you wish to make your priesthood an easy one and at the same time betray it, dispense yourself from seeking those who are estranged and instead wait for them to look for you.[87]

We must go out and look for the people. It is the priest who must make the first move, not the people. It is useless for him to ring his bell. Nobody will listen. It is for him to hear the sirens sounding from the factories, those temples of technical achievement where the modern world lives and breathes. It is for the priest to make of himself a missionary if he would have Christianity endure and become the yeast of civilization.[86]

The priesthood is not a dignity, a power for the advantage of the one who receives it. It is an office of mediation, a priesthood standing between God and man.[88]

You are public men, you exist for society. The day that you forget this, or that you voluntarily refuse to face it, your priesthood will become paralyzed and betrayed. The living of such a relationship with the world has a hundred rules, of which the Church's authority is the sole judge. But of your fidelity to such relationships you are for the most part your own judges.[88]

We are men who are sent. We are missionaries. We are apostles. And the love of God that is communicated to us gives us this thrust, this attraction toward others, which, if we wish to remain faithful, should never die within us so long as there remains even one soul outside the fold of Christ.[87]

People will lay siege to you. People will knock on your doors at all hours of the day or night. People will seek of you what they should not—the goods of this world, or letters of recommendation in order that they may obtain the things of this world that are not yours to give. With these too you must have patience. You must listen to them and show that your love touches even these aspects of their life.[87]

You will find petulant people, indiscreet people, people who are aloof and people who seek to speak to you and to know you. And then you will remember that you are a guide for them; that you have not only duties but rights—and how great they are! [87]

Remember always that the more authority we receive from God the greater is our obligation to serve, that is, to love. May the day never come for us in which our authority is not kind and paternal, understanding and gentle, incapable of triumphing over evil and the importunity of others with the goodness and with the true authority of our ministry wisely employed.[87]

The use of authority, especially the way in which it is used, seems to me to be one of the factors that most draws people today if it is expressed and exercised seriously and kindly. But it can put them to flight if it is expressed in terms of peremptory demand, and if it is rude and imperious.[81]

This lack of courtesy and of moderation is one of the most frequent and pernicious causes of the estrangement of the people from their priests. It indicates a pitiful lack of awareness of the demands of modern thinking, which will not tolerate the abuse of authority, bad treatment, a lack of respect and of good manners. It is also a sign of a serious forgetfulness that the authority of the Church should always be exercised as a paternal service of love to others.[87]

You will find that the normal way of loving others is that of placing yourself at their service, of being at their disposal, of being incapable of saying no, of being in the midst of them not as one who seeks to be served but as one who serves, as our Master has said: "I have not come to be ministered to but I have come to minister." [87]

You will find that this heavy commitment of being the representatives before God of His people obliges you to substitute yourself for them, to assume as Jesus has done all of their failures, their needs, their sins. You must make of yourselves not only the transmitters of the prayers and of the needs of the people of God, but with Christ, victims for them.[87]

You must know how to love, substituting yourself for others, to make your own the burden of their needs and miseries, to be capable, if necessary, of giving also of your life for others.[87]

You will feel yourself different from the world in which you must live, and you will understand why the world looks at you with a kind of amazement and even hostility. But you will be at the same time kind and patient friends of this world that has such need of you.[89]

We all know how this hour of history weighs on souls in a manner such as perhaps in past centuries it never has: in a frenzy of work, of study, of movement, and of thought. Even the good, the Christians, heirs of a tradition which has sanctified them and convinced them that their ultimate destiny is not in time, are fascinated by the vision of the world, by what it offers to the senses, to one's interests, thoughts, study and diversion.[90]

What can be done to reach these people, bound from morning to night by the fever of their own activity, satisfied with the machines they operate, fascinated by their own discoveries, bound by their own laws, attracted by this narrow groove of the earth, which is marvelously productive and allows them to foresee more and more discoveries, more and more creativity? [90]

To break this attraction of people to the world appears extremely difficult. It seems almost as if it should not be done for fear of blocking the design of God, which perhaps is developing under our very eyes.[90]

The hour of the priestly apostolate is not favorable, it is not easy. You will find distracted souls incapable of understanding the spiritual side of things, so prompt to doubt everything, so disposed to rebel against a voice that calls them to God and calls them to the higher vocation of the spirit and of the mysterious and stupendous life of the Church.[90]

You will find so many things that gradually remove themselves from the name of God, from His influence and from His law. They will claim autonomy, they will claim a liberty that speaks often of rebellion and of apostasy, and you will find that this fundamental enmity of the sinful man, of the material man, has become a power— "the power of darkness." [90]

You will meet it in your pastoral work and in your preaching, and you will see that this world of evil and of error is not weak, it is not disorganized and is not occasional, it is not individual. It is strong, it is organized, it is potent, it is aware. The blasphemy that rises against the name of God has become scientific, and logical, and willed. Atheism has become organized and has penetrated everywhere.[90]

Shame to you if you should ever say: "I have taken upon myself the responsibility for this or that form of the apostolate. I limit my activity to what I am capable of doing and to no other." It is necessary to model our priesthood and our sacerdotal action on the needs of others, and not on our own attitudes.[90]

It makes no difference if we cut a bad figure, it makes no difference if we shorten our years and we ruin our health, it makes no difference if we do not have the freedom to take our vacation or to use our time, our days or our years, as we would.[90]

If the Lord demands sacrifice, then let there be sacrifice! [90]

If you seek only yourselves you will live in contradiction. If you seek to give yourself, you will live in harmony with our time and with the genius of this age. We need priests who know truly how to give of themselves, how to multiply themselves, how to draw from themselves the treasures which the Lord has placed in their hearts.[90]

It is necessary to be inexhaustible fountains, necessary to be capable of speaking the language of all and to go everywhere and to respond to all needs. This is the characteristic of our present time.[90]

May this time, which can be so decisive for our people and for history, may it be blessed by God.[90]

If you wish to be effective you must go into the midst of people, you must become their friends and their acquaintances. Your mission will prevail the more vital it becomes, as the relationships you have with those to whom you preach the kingdom and the grace of God become living and personal.[90]

Without this personal involvement the pastoral life of today revolves above the crowd without leaving any impression. This demands much effort and much refining of our instincts. It is not unhuman, however, because it signifies above all that our authority and our dignity become what the Lord wishes: they become service, humility, and friendship. The pastoral life becomes a colloquy, contact of heart to heart, person to person.[90]

The mentality of the modern world is not oriented toward a religion so positive, precise, organized, and demanding as ours. It sympathizes with realities that are not ours; it considers and seeks other goods, which are not those of the Kingdom of God; it feeds other hopes that are not those of Christ.[91]

Yet it is this same modern world that calls for the presence and the action of the Catholic priest, unconsciously perhaps, but with a voice that speaks with lament, that becomes sometimes a cry of anguish or of distracted grief.[91]

The mission of the priest is directed to a world that scorns him and at the same time secretly fears him, envies him, admires him, and desires him.[91]

This is a self-sufficient world. A world proud of itself, capable and rich, a world that wishes to appear contented with itself. It rejects, therefore, as a humiliation and an offense, any denial of its basic sufficiency, any affirmation of its need for prayer, for redemption and for salvation.[91]

The pastoral ministry of today demands not only work, creativity, organizations, and instructions and events. It requires something more intimate, more spiritual and more qualified. So many of our people today await a word that speaks to them of the spirit. They desire not only an external concern for their souls, which creates its own limits, which offers a schedule of service and which imposes a law of service; but they wish above all a transfusion of the spirit.[90]

People have certain charismatic needs, which should

not frighten us, because we know how to satisfy them if we put into our words and into our example something of the authentic quality of our pastoral life.[90]

You, my sons, have become ministers of Christ precisely to weave this colloquy with the modern world that you might be capable of becoming its educators, teachers, spiritual directors and sanctifiers.[92]

We will no longer look at the world under its accidental aspects. We will look at it with eyes of mercy and compassion and once again speak the eternal word of charity and of love. We will have a pasison for souls, we will have a passion for the society that surrounds us, we will have a passion, a love and a charity for all who come to us. They will perhaps scorn us, they will block our way and will perhaps offend us.[92]

But we will not be capable of being offended. The more we love the less we will be loved. The more we love the more difficult will be our task in coming in contact with the world. The more we love the world the more difficult it will be to separate it from its illusions of being happy in itself, sufficient in itself, dependent only on itself.[92]

We will seek with love to overcome all things. We are consecrated men, our charge is sculptured in our souls by the triple character of baptism, of confirmation and of holy orders. It is absorbed by a triple solemn proposition: I will be faithful, I will be zealous, I will be a minister. To forget, to attenuate and to adapt this character to a comfortable, unquestioned mediocrity is to deform our personality. It is to violate the constitutional principles of our being. This is our personal trust.[93]

We are ministers. The day on which we became priests we lost, in a certain sense, every right. The right has passed to the Christian people who must be served: to the poor, to the children, to the ignorant, to the sick, to our adversaries that all may ask and in some measure lay claim on us.[93]

Love is demanding of the one who makes a profession of it. It consumes and it burns. Charity is perfection, it is sanctity. This is our social compact.[93]

We are men of our times. That involves an effort of balance that is critical indeed. We should on the one hand be close, very close to our time. We should know it, approach it, suffer with it, admire it and redeem it. On the other hand we should stand off from it, protect ourselves, isolate ourselves.[93]

From one point of view we should embrace it, from another, immunize ourselves against it. Love and mortification. Service and liberty. In the world yet not of the world.[93]

The world attacks us as antiquated, as formalistic, incapable of understanding it, as badly informed and ridiculous, and it deceives us with misleading equivocations, with apparently innocent naturalness, with false friendship. But then if we yield, it derides us, it scorns us as fatuous, and as salt without savor. What are we to do? [93]

Today, the regular and measured activity of time past is not enough. It is necessary to quicken its pace and to intensify it. This is the tempo of our time and woe to us if we should seek, through love of tradition, to retain the measured pace and tranquil performance of priests of other centuries. The world rushes on. We must quicken our step if we do not wish it to pass us by.[94]

If we are by nature as the rest of men, and if the nature and scope of our ministry obliges us to become brothers to our people on the level of their modest social conditions, we are not, for that reason, similar to others. Our life, our dress, our mentality are different.[94]

Pastoral love is our vocation, it is our obligation, it is our promise. It ought to be our virtue, our art and our speciality.[95]

Pastoral love obliges us to be concerned with the well-being of others, and so we are, with much exterior action which is good and meritorious. However, at times we continue to act no longer by reason of that interior affection which we call zeal, but by reason of a complex of motives, which could be called professional.[95]

It is not always the supernatural love of souls that causes our interest in them. We can be occupied with others by way of habit, legalistic or formal exactness, for fear of reproof or of criticism, for vanity or prestige, for recognition or even, indeed, for self-interest.[95]

Is it possible for example that we, who are priests for the service of others, should declare ourselves unable to render a particular pastoral service? Unable because it costs us dearly; unable because it imposes a fatiguing exercise of preparation, of preaching, of confession, of obedience? [95]

Or is it because it imposes above all the intimate exile of responsibility? [95]

In that case we are constructing first in our imaginations and then by some apparently innocent maneuver a program for our priestly life, a program, rich in ideals if you wish, but where there is also much of one's own taste and perhaps even much for one's own advantage. Little, sometimes even very little, of the spirit of service and of sacrifice, of obedience and of love from which our priesthood had its beginning remains in us.[95]

If it is true that our priesthood is drawn to an always exigent interiority by the very nature of the mystery that it celebrates, it is also true that the priesthood demands a constant expansive exteriorization for the proper exercise of the ministry to which it is dedicated. See then how our life is stretched between two opposing poles, interior silence and exterior action. How can we ever resolve them? [96]

It would be unwise to see, in the importance attributed to the pastoral activity, a forgetfulness, or a rivalry with theological speculation. This speculation maintains its dignity and its excellence even if the impelling necessities of ecclesiastical life demand that sacred doctrine remain not purely speculative but be cultivated in the complete context of the Christian economy. It must be doctrine which is given to us that we may live the true religion, announce it to souls, and demonstrate its saving virtue in the historical reality of our time.[97]

He who is a shepherd, a seeker after the lost sheep, must never forget, diminish or deny the patrimony of truth which is his to communicate. Not only must the truth be preserved intact, but the moral conduct of the shepherd as well. He should never alter the true and austere stamp of his priestly character.[81]

It is true that to draw near to others it is necessary to become in some way one with them, "rejoice with the rejoicing, weep with those who weep," but this should not mean that harm should be done to the genuine spirit and form of the priesthood. He who diminishes himself by making his own the worldly forms of the surroundings in which he expects to exercise his ministry, weakens his moral impact. He exposes himself to the danger of adopting the way of thinking of others rather than of imposing his own, and sometimes raises the question of what degree is his virtue and of his sincerity.[81]

The drama of the priest workers was aggravated by this excessive process of assimilation of the priest into the secular context. The result was that many who entered it with apostolic generosity became its material as well as its spiritual prisoners.[81]

The priest who is involved with the world will not become a part of it. He is in it to explore with those he encounters the path of belief and of return. It is a way that is full of peril. But we should not make of it a difficult and bitter one for the fellow priest who explores new fields, be it in the cinema, in literature, the press, art, sport, assistance to workers, the military, immigrants, or prisoners, when his superior has authorized it and prudence and charity are his guides.[81]

Too often in the past the cry of scandal has been raised when some zealous pastor has sought to explore a new and courageous path.[81]

Risk is an essential element in the pastoral art.[81]

If we do not want the pastoral art to be paralyzed at the moment of birth, we should, with a broad perspective, allow pastoral experimentation. We should assist it, and give it direction until such time as it will have proved or disproved its validity.[81]

The word *aggiornamento,* which my predecessor John XXIII used himself and which he inserted in the program of the Ecumenical Council, when applied to the ecclesiastical field, is a word that indicates the relationship between the eternal values of Christian truth and their insertion in the dynamic reality of human life which is today so extraordinarily capricious. It is, too, in our present uneasy, disturbed times, a word that is continually and variously modifying itself.[97]

It is the word that indicates the relative and experimental aspect of the ministry of salvation, which desires above all a significant success, and which knows how much its efficiency is conditioned by the social, moral, and cultural state of the souls to whom it is directed. It knows also how favorable to social well-being but especially to the practical increase of the apostolate it is to know the experiences of others and to make the good in them one's own.[97]

It is a word which shows a repugnance for customs that have been bypassed, for the tired ways that hold one back, for incomprehensible forms, for neutralizing distances, for the presumptuous and uncomprehending ignorance concerning new human phenomena, as indeed for scant faith in the enduring actuality and fertility of the Gospel.[97]

It is a word that can seem fawningly deferential to what is capricious and flighty, as to an existentialism without belief in transcendental objective values, and desirous only of a momentary and subjective fulfillment. But it is instead a word that assigns due importance to the rapid and inexorable succession of phenomena to which life is witness, and seeks to associate itself with the celebrated recommendation of the Apostle, "hoarding the opportunity which is given you in evil times like these." [97]

It is a word, indeed, that we receive with pleasure as

the expression of a love desirous of rendering testimony to the perennial and therefore modern vitality of the priestly ministry.[97]

And while we are on this subject, we should give a warm welcome to another term. That word is pastoral. Today it is a programmatic and glorious word. The Ecumenical Council has made it its own and centered in it its reforming and renewing intention. There is no need to see in this adjective, when applied to the most characteristic manifestations of ecclesiastical life, an inadvertent but harmful yielding to the activism of our times. It need not be exercised at the expense of the interior life and of contemplation, which should always have primacy in our religious values. Such a primacy remains even if in practice the apostolic demands of the Kingdom of God in the complexity of contemporary life demand a priority of time and of energy in the service of charity.[97]

I know well what apprehensions often weigh down the heart of a bishop, what sufferings afflict him, not so much because of the lack of means, grave and preoccupying though they be, but because of the deafness of those who should hear his word; the diffidence that envelops and isolates him; the indifference and lack of esteem that seem to obstruct his ministry and to paralyze it.[97]

I know how many parish priests and their assistants care for souls in areas that are vast and populous, where the number, the mentality and the demands of the inhabitants oblige them to unceasing and exhausting work. I know also how many priests must exercise their ministry hidden away in small villages lacking the joy of genuine conversation, of collaboration, and of comforting results.[97]

Many of them are often living in worrisome economic conditions, often opposed and misunderstood and obliged to live turned in on themselves, finding their consolation in the humble who surround them, their breviary, and in the tabernacled Mystery of the Divine Presence.[97]

I feel obliged to assure these dear and beloved brothers, tireless workers for the Gospel, modest and faithful ministers of the Church of God, that I think of them, understand them, esteem them, assist them, love them, and follow them with my prayers and with my blessing.[97]

XIX

THE SISTER IN THE MODERN WORLD

THERE COMES to my mind the Gospel figures who have gone before you in your vocation. I see, in the scenes from the Gospel, those first silent followers who accompanied our Lord in His apostolic journeys. "They followed Him, they ministered to Him, and they helped Him by means of alms." [98]

The Church of God sees you, now and always, as its most beloved daughters who strive to be pious, devout and faithful. It sees you as women who have taken the words of Christ seriously and have given yourselves to Him, have given up everything at His word and have answered His call.[98]

Something that has always struck me as wonderful is this aspect of your service in the world. As the state of consecration evolved and assumed different forms, it did not change the preceding forms, but absorbed them. From the consecration of individual virgins, it came to encompass a group, but the consecration remained the same. The cloistered way of life remained with all its rules and regulations, its austerity, asceticism, discipline, obedience, and mortification. The religious state remained, but it was brought out into the world.[98]

And thus we have Sisters living in the world, Sisters who are everywhere but who have taken to themselves all of the ascetic development and discipline of perfection that the centuries have taught the women dedicated to Christ.[98]

It is to this point that I have wished to lead you. What is your place in the world today? I remember having had the good fortune to be near His Holiness, Pius XII, when he spoke inspiring words to you, words that you would do well to know and remember. I remember having heard him express these thoughts. "The Sisters must be called to become collaborators." "Even the cloistered ones?" "Yes, even those." "But shouldn't they stay behind the grill?" "Behind the grill if they wish, but they, too, have their contribution to make." [98]

Therefore, the Church of God calls to religious women, because its need demands that they come closer to the pastoral life, to the priesthood, where the responsibility and mission of saving souls resides.[98]

Yet while you live, making of your rule, your discipline, and your constitutions a way of life, I see that your religious state, which is usually more conservative than that of men, is marked by a certain dynamism, a certain movement. There is among you an evolution, a development, a transformation. In which direction does it tend? [98]

You have given of yourselves in education, in the service of the sick, in schools, and in hospitals. And now the Church says: "There is more to be asked of you. You are capable of doing more. I want you closer. I will break up your ranks. I will separate you into little groups. I will scatter you among the Christian people, who have such need of seeing consecrated virgins in their midst. I will place you before the eyes of society, especially its youth, who have no other example of a life of virtue and of complete offering. I will put you close to my parishes. I will call you closer to my altars, I will involve you in all my activity for the salvation and sanctification of the world." [98]

This is the modern vocation of the Sister—to become a collaborator in the pastoral action of the Church. You are called to save souls, and not only by caring for the sick or by educating children.[98]

You are called to become today co-workers in this supreme act of love, that of the priest—the charity of one willing to become a pastor of souls. You are called to give up every reason (egotism or incapacity, for example) that you might have for wanting to seclude yourselves, in order to become collaborators; the humblest, possibly, but also the most devoted, and the most necessary.[98]

It sometimes happens that the "sense of the Church," the being attuned to the mind of the Church, is somewhat diminished and less cultivated in certain religious families. It happens by way of their living in seclusion and in finding in their communities all the objects of their concern, knowing or caring little about what is happening outside the enclosure of their occupations, to which they are totally dedicated.[116]

Become also—and now I use the ancient word—become the "deaconesses" of the Church of Christ. Become, that is, the ministers of its needs. You must come closer to the altar, to souls, to the Church in which are gathered together the people of God.[98]

Do not refuse this vocation! [98]

A modern parish cannot do without the Sisters. You have become more necessary today than yesterday because in the past it was enough for you to remain within your monasteries, within your convents. Today, you must give up this comfort, this tranquillity. Now you will be plunged into the midst of the life of the citizens of the cities of the world. You will become, in your little cloisters, in your little groups, the salt of the earth and the light of the world, as are our priests. You will truly become the collaborators of the Church, which seeks to sanctify and save the world.[98]

I speak to you from the heart. The mission I point out will give you innumerable annoyances and worries because the apostolate, the service of souls, is sacrifice, not comfort. It will make you even poorer than before. It will make you capable of a poverty that will be lived, not merely professed.[98]

It will place you in direct contact with modern humanity so starved by life, and so in need of being purified and saved. You have left the sinful world, only in order to come closer to it! [98]

You will see, from close range, what sin is, what the malice of the world is, and what the work of Satan is in souls. You will have to learn to struggle face to face against this mysterious presence of evil in the world. Try, my dear Sisters, try to understand this modern vocation of the religious state! And I add a second recommendation: prepare yourselves for it! [98]

You must become qualified in all areas of your activity and intellectual formation, so that you will be able on every level, to influence, to educate, and to Christianize the world. Prepare yourselves; and see to it that you carry through, even though it will disturb and upset your daily program, and will change some of your customs.[98]

I do not promise you that you will be happy in this world. You have already renounced this kind of joy. It may be that the Cross of Christ will lie heavier on your shoulders and that you may also be called to suffer, as is true in so many countries where Christ is rejected. Perhaps you will also be asked to offer those sacrifices that persecution knows how to inflict on the most faithful witnesses of the Gospels. But, even in this, rejoice, for it is the eighth beatitude: "Blessed are you when men reproach you, and persecute you, and, speaking falsely, say all manner of evil against you, for My sake. Rejoice and exult, because your reward is great in heaven." [98]

XX

GOD'S NEED FOR MAN

I ADDRESS MYSELF to those who profess monotheism and who with us pay religious worship to the one true God, the living and supreme God, the God of Abraham, the Most High.[40]

We Christians, taught by revelation, know that God subsists in three Persons, Father, Son, and Holy Ghost, but we always extol the divine nature as being one, we announce as one the living and true God. To those who worship the one God go my wishes for peace in justice.[40]

I am the representative and the promoter of the Christian religion. I have the certainty of promoting a cause which comes from God. I am the disciple, the apostle, the missionary of Jesus, Son of God and the Son of Mary, the Messiah, the Christ. I continue His mission, I am the herald of His message, I am the minister of His religion, which we know possesses all the divine guarantees of truth.[40]

My salutation recognizes no boundaries. It surmounts all barriers and reaches out to men of good will, including those who, at the moment, do not show good will towards the religion of Christ, and who strive to prevent its spread and interfere with those who believe in it. Even

232

to those who persecute Catholicism and who deny God
and Christ I send my sorrowful remembrance and I ask
them calmly: "Why? Why?" [40]

I am determined to place those estranged from us in
the forefront of my activity and my prayer. If there is a
voice that can reach you, those of you who have left the
Church, the first will be one that asks pardon of you.
Yes, I of you. When I see one who has fallen away, there
is much remorse. Why is this brother estranged from me?
Because he has not been sufficiently loved. [53]

I refer to the Hebrew people, faithful as they are to the
religion which we call that of the Old Testament. Remembered, too, are those adorers of God, according to the
concept of monotheism, especially the Moslems, deserving as they all are of our admiration for all that is true
and good in their worship of God, and finally, the followers of the great Afro-Asiatic religions. [115]

I am moved by the pastoral office which I hold to seek
in the heart of the modern atheist also the motives of his
turmoil and denial. [115]

His motives are many and complex. He is a man full
of yearning, prompted sometimes by passion and desire
for the unattainable, but often also by great-hearted
dreams of justice and progress. [115]

Sometimes, too, the atheist is spurred on by noble sentiments and by impatience with the mediocrity and self-
seeking of so many contemporary social settings. He
knows well how to borrow from our Gospel modes and
expressions of solidarity and human compassion. Will we
know one day how to lead him too to the Christian source
of such expressions of moral worth? [115]

I look at the world with enormous sympathy. If the

world feels itself to be estranged from Christianity, Christianity does not feel a stranger to the world, no matter under what aspect it presents itself, or the content of its address.[40]

May the world realize that it is esteemed and loved. It is a love that our faith places in the heart of all the Church, that does nothing other than transmit the immense and marvelous love that God has for man.[40]

The mission of Christianity is one of friendship for humanity, a mission of understanding, encouragement, advancement and of elevation. I say it again; it is one of salvation.[40]

The wisdom of which the Church is the guardian and instructor, has this adage: *"Homo sum, et nihil humani a me alienum puto,"* "I am a man, and nothing that is human is foreign to me." On any topic that concerns man, his life, his soul, his destiny, the Church has a word of wisdom to speak.[34]

Face to face with his most powerful creations and even in comparison to the universe which is opening its mysteries to him, man remains first in importance. Man is for us the supreme value in the visible world. And as the concern for man's physical health, exposed to the hazards and shocks of flight in the atmosphere and in space, is not considered as a restraint on his conquering urge, but as a help, in the same way the Church's concern for the spiritual and moral well-being of man must not be considered as an obstacle. Rather it is a protection, a guarantee, a help in man's conquest of his ultimate destiny.[99]

It is well known that the Church regards scientific progress and the professional growth which flows from it with admiration, sympathy, and confidence. This optimistic attitude on the Church's part stems from its religious conception of the world: that where there is research, discovery, conquest, development of knowledge and of activity, there is a development of human capacities. There is, as well, a penetration of the work of God, a use of the resources which it embraces, and consequently a drawing closer of the two parties involved: man and God.[100]

It is for this reason that I believe that scientific progress, far from making religion useless, prepares and makes possible the most profound and sublime expressions of this relationship. Today, this tending of the scientific world towards an ultimate and transcendent recognition of religion is beginning to penetrate the most reflective minds.[100]

One can only hope that it is a prelude to a new canticle of creatures, completely different from that of Saint Francis of Assisi. The latter is all candor and beauty, but this new canticle, because it is to be rational and mathematical, will not, for all that, be less lyrical and mystical.[100]

For Everyman I have a message which I believe is one of liberation. And I presume to suggest it to him because it is completely human. It is the message of Man to man. The Christ Whom we offer to mankind is the "Son of Man," as He called Himself. He is the first-born, the prototype of the new mankind. He is the brother, companion, and friend of all. Of Him alone can it be said in all truth that "He knows all there is in man." He is sent by God, but it is not to condemn the world but to save it.[40]

He is the good shepherd of mankind. There is no human value that He has not respected, elevated, and ransomed.

There is no human suffering that He has not understood, shared and ennobled. There is no human need, other than moral imperfection, that He has not assumed and experienced in Himself, and suggests to the restlessness and hearts of men as an object of their interest and love and as a condition of their own salvation.[40]

Even for evil, which, as the physician of mankind He knew and denounced with unflagging vigor, He had an infinite mercy, to the point of making rise in man's heart, by means of grace, the true sources of redemption and life.[40]

May it be known by the world how Christ, Who is living still today in His Church, shows Himself to the world beginning here in Bethlehem, from the crib that marked His appearance on earth.[40]

God's plan for the world is realized in Jesus Christ. The mystery of the redemption of mankind, hidden for long ages, is openly revealed: in Christ we are saved. Our destiny depends on Christ, our problems find their solution in Christ, in Christ our sorrows have meaning.[40]

Christ is our total hope.[40]

The Lord's Resurrection is not an isolated fact, it is a fact which concerns the whole of mankind. From Christ it extends to the world; it has a cosmic importance. And what a source of wonder it is! [40]

That tremendous event affects all men born into this world, with diverse and dramatic consequences. It permeates the whole family tree of mankind. Christ is the new Adam, who infuses into the frail, mortal organism of natural human life a vital new principle, which is real, though too great for words to express. It is a principle of purifying rebirth, a seed of immortality, a link of living communion with Him, the Christ. Through it we share with Him, in the unity of the Holy Spirit, in the very life of the infinite God, Whom we can in our happiness call our Father. And again this is because of Christ.[40]

It is on the reality of Christ's Resurrection that the religion that takes its name and life from Him is founded. And the light, the strength, the happiness and the holiness that are born of faith in Him are such that the Christian religion offers not only fulness of peace and joy to whoever professes it from his heart, but radiates such an invitation, awakens such a desire, and stirs up such a restlessness, as to keep the question of religion ever alive in the world.[40]

It is true that the Christian life is austere; it is no stranger to pain and self-denial. It demands penance and sacrifice. It accepts the Cross, and when the time comes, bravely goes out to meet suffering and death.[10]

But in its essential manifestation Christian life is happiness. Recall the program of life laid down by Christ in the discourse on the beatitudes. You will see that it is essentially positive. Christian life is a force that liberates, purifies, and transforms. Everything is reduced to the good, to joy, in Christian living.[10]

It is human. But it is more than human, for it is permeated by the life-giving presence of the Spirit, the consoler, the spirit of Christ, Who comforts and sustains it and gives it the power to perform higher acts of believing, of hoping, and of loving. It is supremely optimistic and creative. It enjoys happiness today in expectation of perfect happiness tomorrow.[10]

Our confidence, our adherence to the Church's teaching and its discipline does not make our thoughts sterile nor estrange them from an understanding and an acquiring of what modern knowledge possesses and produces. It is a confidence that comes from having at hand arguments and reasons for confronting the intellectual and spiritual manifestations of our times in a dialogue that is both faithful and productive. With it comes the assurance of being stimulated to make the fullest possible use of new expressions of thought and language, since the riches of truth that the faith guarantees in the divine and religious sphere are ever fresh and living.[34]

The spread of the message of salvation is not done ordinarily by virtue of the message itself, as often happens with human ideas and scientific truths, but comes about by virtue of a human ministry. It is spread by way of preaching, of testimony, and of tradition, by way of the apostolate.[101]

The salvation-economy of Christianity is bound to a human work that associates man with God, the minister with Christ, and the apostle with the Saviour. This dependence of the divine plan on human collaboration constitutes the mystery of the apostolicity of Christianity.[101]

Christianity becomes universal by way of the apostolate. Catholicity is realized by means of apostolic effort, of missionary dynamism.[101]

The habitual use of words often weakens their force and the import of their meaning. We use with careless facility the word catholic, almost without noticing the fulness it embraces, the dynamic it generates, the beauty it reveals, the commitment it imposes. It often becomes in common use a defining term, and thus something which circumscribes and limits the Church to distinguish it from other divisions, worthy of respect and endowed with immense Christian treasures, yet separate from the Catholic fulness.[111]

Today all are called to be apostles and missionaries. The social and spiritual crisis of the world on the one hand, and the maturing of particular situations in the world itself, which seem to be a prelude to its ultimate peace and unity, call the Christian to a responsibility of active testimony of his faith.[101]

A happy Christianity, a comfortable Christianity, a possibly useful Christianity, is still the concept that many have of religion. They seek to reduce its profession to accustomed forms, intermittently expressed and almost insignificant in content. These Christians, if they are indeed still Christians, do not think of professing their faith in such a way that others may have its example and comfort. Having lowered in themselves the flame of wisdom and of coherence that is the faith, they do not object nor hesitate to project a dark shadow on those who instead expect from them a consoling reflection of the light. That interior light must be rekindled.[101]

The appearance of Christ generates a vocation in the world. The appearance of Christ gives birth to a responsibility.[47]

The coming of Christ ought to provoke a dynamism of thought and of life such as to shake the position of passivity of the faithful and of those who are not of the Church. Immobilism is no longer justifiable.[47]

A zeal that expresses charity, and that seeks to institute a search for methods suited to the new forms of life, and to prepare and maintain a dialogue with the modern world, is an effort to bring the world to Christ, in Whom all things are re-established and find their completion.[43]

Such an effort is praiseworthy, since it does not seek to disown the historic past. Neither does it seek to break with traditions in their essential and venerated intent, but rather it pays tribute to them. To make them vital, however, and to preserve their effectiveness, it may be necessary to prune them of what is transitory and worn, of any stupendous realities of religion.[54]

Unhappily, there often does not exist much difference between the concept of life that so many Christians have and that possessed by those who are not aware of the stupendous realities of religion.[55]

The Christian is not in reality, and ought not to be in practice, like the man who does not have the good fortune to be a Christian. The Christian ought to be set off from the mundane and pagan customs which surround him. The Christian should know how to immunize himself against the irreligious and immoral life that the world, ignorant of God and of Christ, creates about him. He ought to give his own life a dignity and a moral style, which the man who is not Christian is often tempted to deride and to proclaim impossible.[102]

One of the great evils of our time is precisely this: that Christians are not Christians, and that the mystery of newness and continuity communicated to them in the baptism of resurrection is not lived by them. In its place are compromise, inconsistency, lack of logic and infidelity. These are the miserable survivals of a vocation which should have embraced perfection, sanctity, and Christian fulness.[5]

Unfortunately none of us—with the exception of a few saints—is immune to the conformism that, though maintaining the appearances of Christian obligation, diminishes it and sometimes suppresses its demands.[5]

Nothing is easier—and contemporary literature proves it—than to criticize those who are "practicing" Catholics, and those who are consecrated to the service and the imitation of Christ. To discover moral defects and contradictions in those who follow the Christian message is easier the more that teaching is not simply a name but a reality, the more exigent it is in its demands on those who embrace it.[5]

Thus no one escapes a certain inconsistency between the name of Christian that he bears and his non-Christian way of living.[5]

While the Christian participates in every worthy manifestation of life and is indeed the first to promote, sustain, and sanctify it, he cannot be indifferent to the moral value of the things which surround him. He is sincere and severe in giving them the elementary but fundamental qualification of good or bad according to their merit. He is, at the same time, an optimist who believes in the good, who believes in virtue. He discovers and strengthens it also in those not yet perfect. He defends it with his word and example and seeks to live it sincerely within himself.[102]

We Christians live in the presence of God, we are immersed in His law, and when we lie—that is, when we perform actions outside His law—our disorder wounds the immanent order of things, that order that is above and beyond us.[15]

I think that today this is important for us who are Christians. We ought to give to this title a fuller and more consistent content. Our Christianity ought to derive from its supernatural roots, which are faith and grace, a clearer and stronger expression.[102]

Too often our Christianity is simply nominal and formal: it is then that it reacts against us. It becomes a heavy burden when we seek to sustain it as a merely traditional observance. It becomes responsibility and not energy. It becomes a source of accusation against us on the part of so many who see it in us as dead, unobserved and perhaps betrayed.[102]

To call oneself a Christian without following Christ is an act of derision directed against divine truth and human intelligence.[103]

The mystical newness of Christianity demands and produces a new asceticism. The Christian will always be in the process of renewal. He will never rest in an acquired grade of virtue, but he will seek always for a higher and better one. He will always have before him a model of perfection; the more challenging to imitate, the more unattainable its realization.[55]

The concept of spiritual and moral newness introduced by the newness of the Gospel and especially by the fact of the Resurrection of Christ is a dynamic one. It moves souls, it creates saints, and gives Christian society a continuous and reforming thrust, an unsatisfied aspiration towards a higher order, a burning and trusting desire for the sure attainment of a good—which is realized in the very moment that man begins to seek it with good will.[55]

The heart of man of itself is small, it is egoistic. It has no room except for himself and a handful of others—his family, his caste; even when, after long, noble, and wearisome effort, he arrives at some understanding of his own nation and social class, he is still searching for barriers and confines within which to take measure and refuge.[111]

The manner of Christian witness in our society and in conversation with particular sects and individuals can and should change. It should bring itself up to date, and more in line with the forms and languages of people to-day.[101]

But I would ask all who are engaged in such witness and dialogue to avoid the two perils to which the commitment of their apostolate is open. The first is maintaining as ingenuous, devotional, and superfluous a continual return to the motives that have generated and even now justify such effort as theirs—that is, fidelity to Christ and to the Church, moral intransigence and reasons of charity. This is a spiritual patrimony to which we ought not only to give a kind of ideological subscription, but from which we should always draw the breath of our thought and the vigor of our action.[101]

The dialogue, the necessary method of the apostolate, should not terminate in a negation or in a forgetfulness of truth to the enrichment of error or of the partial truth it may be seeking to redeem.[101]

It is the equivocal that tempts us in this area. It could perhaps drain the Catholic affirmation and dilute it in a hybrid syncretism of ideas and methods, and condition the Catholic apostle to a kind of opportunistic and servile conformity.[101]

Salt without its savor serves no purpose.[101]

It is not always the star of certitude that lights our path, but it should be enough to have seen it just once in order

to continue on the way it indicates. We have a hunger
for it, especially in some periods of our life, the younger
years especially.[101]

But it is not always given to us to experience this
charism of truth, and this is especially true of that truth
that derives its certainty not from intrinsic evidence but
from authority, and from the stupendous but delicate interplay of our spiritual and superior faculties, which we call
the faith, a gift to our brothers and a light to society.[104]

Together with the Gospel I repeat: Our faith is truth.
It is real, complete and one. You cannot prescind from it.
To exclude faith—religion—is like wanting to deprive
oneself of the light from the sun, of air for breathing, of
bread for eating.[104]

Our faith is the beginning of a new life. The word I
would like to have stamped on your souls, above all the
souls of young people where this spiritual challenge can be
the most real and also the most dangerous, is the necessary word: faith. Our faith is necessary, it is *necessary*.
Without faith in Christ our life does not have its true interpretation, its just epilogue. Separated from the faith, one
might seem to have, at first glance, a greater freedom, a
quicker and more responsive dynamism. It would be instead a race toward the abyss of misery, toward destinies
of deep and irreparable tragedy.[105]

Our faith is our certainty. It is our foundation. It is our
light, our comfort, our hope. It will be, tomorrow, our
happiness.[105]

There may be some who say: "But if I choose Christ, if
I remain faithful to my belief, I lose the earth. I ignore my
economic interests. I cancel my liberty. I will have no
longer the mastery of the world that the Kingdom of God

seems to challenge." But to quiet and to reassure us there is the divine word of the Saviour. It is always a question of putting the faith, religious and spiritual values, in first place; as when I turn on the overhead light in my room in order that everything may be illuminated.[105]

Nothing that is truly honest, good, and vital will be lost, since the word of our Lord reassures us: "Seek you first the Kingdom of God and all things will be added unto you." This means that when we give to our religious life its primacy, and we recognize the role of the worship of God and the love of Christ and fidelity to the Church in our life, we will not lose anything of what our life needs.[105]

I would like all to realize that the elevation of the individual to the sacred and inviolable dignity of a person charged with the vocation and the splendor of the sons of God and brothers in Christ is the mission of our religion. It preserves and defends in every human being his stature of nobility and greatness, and raises it to a high degree of supernatural life.[106]

This is a marvelous thing that can be wrought by the Christian religion. It is effected by allowing the social phenomena of the modern world (which produces organizations that virtually absorb and almost annihilate the individual) to develop in accord with the normal laws of progress. But it also penetrates these phenomena, and infuses them with the inalienable principles of respect for the human person. Thus it ennobles and even sanctifies him.[106]

I remind you of this function of the religious life, which enters into economic, professional and social activity, so that you will not entertain the delusion, unfortunately widespread in contemporary public thought, that technical

progress is sufficient for our life, and that it can replace
all that was once attributed to providence, to the spiritual
life and to religious faith.[106]

Your intelligence should strengthen your conviction
that, the greater our technical progress, the more urgent
the duty and the necessity to be faithful to religion. The
more our machine civilization engulfs the life of man, in
the very act of serving him, the more we must feed the
life of the spirit which prayer and faith alone can do.[106]

This process of understanding and reassessing religion
as a significant and necessary element of life is not always
easy. The Church should periodically review its methods
of presenting the message of Christ. The faithful, indeed
every intelligent and responsible person, should support
this effort of *"aggiornamento,"* as it is now called.[106]

I would like to encourage you, in your good will, not
to despair, and not to give way to the temptation of super-
ficiality, not to deprive yourselves of the joy of discovering how Christianity, which seems ancient and superfluous
to those absorbed in the experience of contemporary life,
is, instead, vital and beautiful, and, one might say, designed
especially for our century and for the real problems of our
spirit.[106]

If you ask if it is possible, it is enough for us to remember how the human face of Christ hides and, at the same
time, reveals His divine face. How Jesus, and with Him
Christianity, appears to us with features that often at first
sight do not show anything extraordinary, original, or profound.[106]

In fact, at times the face of Christ is that of a man who
suffers, Who has been condemned, the face of a dead man.

We hear again the heartbreaking words of Isaiah that refer to the crucified Christ: "No stateliness here, no majesty, no beauty as we gaze upon Him, to win our hearts. Here is one despised, left out of all human reckoning; bowed with misery, and no stranger to weakness; how should we recognize that face?" [106]

The face of Christ and that of His religion appear to us at times wretched and pitiable, the very mirror of human infirmity and distortion. It can seem strained, profaned, and incapable of communicating what is so much appreciated today—sensible beauty, the dignified expression, the joyous appearance. [106]

It seems deprived of any inner light, no longer beautiful and shining under the artificial lights of human cleverness, which lure and dazzle the eyes of our younger generation. Yet it seems too that it is deprived of its own light by those who should make it shine and raise it high and consolingly above the human scene. [106]

This is to say, that Christ and His Church do not seem to have any attraction for us, no secret with which to fascinate us and save us. [106]

We must rediscover the transfigured face of Christ to feel that He is still, and especially for us, our light. He is the light that illuminates every soul that seeks Him and receives Him. He throws light on every human scene, on every human effort, lending it color and meaning, worth and purpose, hope and happiness. [106]

And finally, the universality of Christianity tells us that it is not a chimera to look to the future transformation of the spiritual panorama of the world. We are conditioned to consider it subdivided into fixed zones of religion, of civilizations, of social and political regimes, zones impenetrable to Christianity, unresponsive to the Catholic vocation, unyielding before the Church.[101]

But if Christianity is not a privilege for some but a gift for all, if Catholicism is a divine program in the world, if the Church is not a particular sect of the spiritual family of humanity, we may also hope that one day all people and perhaps also all men will participate in singing a hymn of glory and of peace.[101]

It is my hope. It is a hope for the world.[101]

REFERENCES

1. Discourse to Extraordinary Missions, Rome, June 24, 1963.
2. Coronation Speech, Rome, June 29, 1963.
3. First Radio Message to the World, Rome, June 22, 1963.
4. Sermon, Cathedral of Frascati, September 1, 1963.
5. Easter Sermon, Milan, 1956.
6. Address to Diplomatic Corps, Sistine Chapel, July 1, 1963.
7. Address before the Celebration of Mass for Milanese and Brescian Citizens, Saint Charles on the Corso, Rome, June 29, 1963.
8. *The Religious Sense,* Pastoral Letter, Milan, 1957.
9. *The Moral Sense,* Pastoral Letter, Milan, 1961.
10. Easter Message, Rome, 1964.
11. Message to Archdiocese of Milan, Rome, August, 1963.
12. *Semaines Sociales de France,* 1963.
13. Sermon for Monday of Holy Week, Milan, 1959.
14. *The Christian and Temporal Well-Being,* Lenten Pastoral, Milan, 1963.
15. Sermon for Tuesday of Holy Week, Milan, 1959.
16. Sermon for Wednesday of Holy Week, Milan, 1959.

17. Sermon for Wednesday of Holy Week, Milan, 1961.
18. Sermon for Tuesday of Holy Week, Milan, 1961.
19. Christmas Sermon, Milan, 1959.
20. Address to the Association for the Study of World Problems of Refugees, Rome, October 3, 1963.
21. Good Friday Homily, Rome, 1964.
22. Gospel Homily, Albano, August 22, 1963.
23. Christmas Sermon, Milan, 1958.
24. Christmas Sermon, Milan, 1957.
25. Christmas Message, Rome, 1963.
26. Christmas Homily to Diplomatic Corps, Rome, December 28, 1963.
27. Speech at Vigorelli Stadium, Milan, June 1, 1963.
28. Discourse to Participants in UN Conference on Tourism, Castelgandolfo, August 31, 1963.
29. Audience of Secretary-General of United Nations U Thant, Rome, July 11, 1963.
30. Telegram to President Kennedy, Prime Minister MacMillan, Premier Khrushchev, and Secretary-General U Thant, July 22, 1963.
31. Address to Congress for European Unity, Rome, November 9, 1963.
32. Address to Young Christian Workers, Rome, March 6, 1964.
33. Discourse to the Youth of the Organization for European Economic Community, Rome, July 23, 1963.
34. Discourse to Catholic University Students at Close of Thirty-Seventh Congress at Padua, Rome, September 3, 1963.
35. Discourse to Slovak Pilgrims, Rome, September 14, 1963.
36. Letter to Italian Catholic Social Week, Rome, September, 1953.
37. Greeting to Nigerian Catholics Visiting Rome, June, 1963.

38. Allocution to Diplomatic Corps in Sistine Chapel, July 1, 1963.
39. Sermon for the Epiphany, Milan, 1959.
40. Sermon for the Epiphany, Bethlehem, 1964.
41. Religion and Labor, Address to the Workers of the World, Turin, 1960.
42. Address to Workers, Sesto San Giovanni, January 19, 1955.
43. Letter to Spanish Workers, Rome, March 26, 1964.
44. *The Christian Family,* Pastoral Letter, Milan, 1960.
45. Address to Meeting of Italian Federation of Church Schools, Milan, 1958.
46. Christmas, Milan, 1960.
47. Epiphany, Milan, 1956.
48. Christmas, Milan, 1961.
49. Epiphany, Milan, 1958.
50. Epiphany, Milan, 1957.
51. General Audience, November 6, 1963.
52. The Cathedral, Milan, 1956.
53. Christians Are the Soul of the World. Discourse to Milanese Catholic Action, October 15, 1961.
54. Sermon for Holy Week, Saturday, 1959.
55. Easter, 1958.
56. Easter, 1959.
57. Easter, 1960.
58. Easter, 1961.
59. Radio Message, Mission of Milan, 1957.
60. Address to Apostolate of the Laity, Rome, 1957.
61. Address to Course in Christian Studies, Assisi, August 29, 1960.
62. Mission to Florence, November 10, 1960.
63. Address to the College of Cardinals, December 24, 1963.
64. *Liturgical Formation,* Pastoral Letter, Milan, 1958.

87. Ordination Address, Milan, June 28, 1957.
88. Ordination Address, Milan, February 25, 1961.
89. Ordination Address, Milan, June 21, 1958.
90. Ordination Address, Milan, June 28, 1959.
91. Ordination Address, Milan, June 28, 1961.
92. Ordination Address, Milan, March 10, 1963.
93. Letter to Clergy, Feast of the Annunciation, Milan, 1963.
94. Letter to Clergy, Palm Sunday, Milan, 1959.
95. Letter to Clergy, Palm Sunday, Milan, 1961.
96. Letter to Clergy, Palm Sunday, Milan, 1962.
97. Address at Castelgandolfo to Priests Participating in Eighth National Week of Pastoral Orientation, held in Orvieto, September 6, 1963.
98. Discourse to Sisters, Milan, February 11, 1961.
99. Address to Congress of Aeronautical and Space Medicine, Rome, October 5, 1963.
100. Address to Congress of Oral Surgeons, Rome, October 29, 1963.
101. Epiphany, Milan, 1960.
102. Saturday of Holy Week, 1961.
103. Christmas, 1956.
104. Epiphany, 1961.
105. Discourse in Parish Church, Genzano, September 8, 1963.
106. Address to Telephone Workers, February 29, 1964.
107. Sermon, Lady of Lourdes Church, Rome, February 23, 1964.
108. Letter to Patriarch Athenagoras, April 18, 1964.
109. Apostolic Letter, *Spiritus Paracliti,* April 30, 1964.
110. Address, Italian Union of Artists, Sistine Chapel, May 7, 1964.
111. Address announcing establishment of Secretariat for Non-Christian Religions, Rome, Pentecost, May 17, 1964.